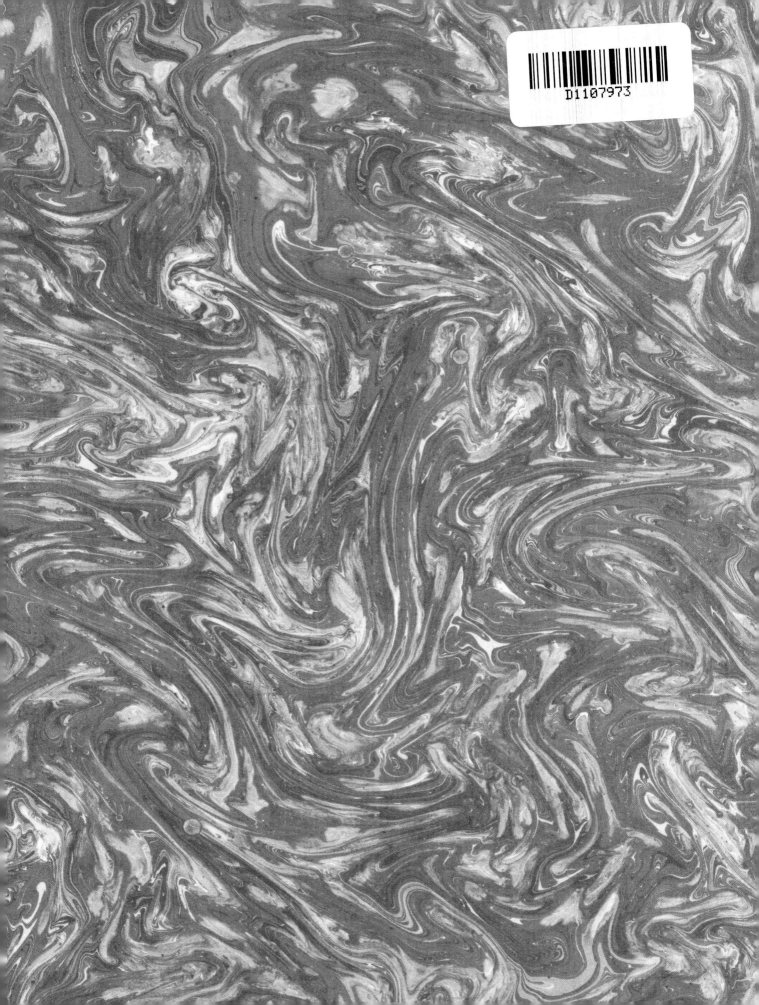

HERITAGE
OF
GOLD

The First 100 Years of
Sunkist Growers, Inc.
1893 -1993

TABLE OF CONTENTS

———

TABLE OF CONTENTS

The Sunkist executive stood looking out over the sprawling city of Tokyo. Below him, the streets were congested with traffic, the sidewalks filled with an unending stream of people. He watched as they walked to their offices, to the subways, to the city's shops and stores. On the tallest buildings, huge signs several stories tall advertised the names of companies from Kodak to Canon, from Mitsubishi to McDonald's.

From Russell Hanlin's viewpoint, the most important name of all couldn't be seen. Yet the Sunkist president knew it was there, in letters only a few millimeters high. All over the city, in grocery stores and restaurants everywhere, the Sunkist label was stamped or stickered on millions of the world's best oranges and lemons.

It was 1993, and Japan had become the citrus company's largest foreign customer. Getting there hadn't been easy, Hanlin thought, but then, not many things had been easy for a long, long time. In fact, as he thought about it, Sunkist had faced constant struggle from the very beginning. But time and time again, the cooperative had come through the fire of doing business with a perishable commodity. Somehow, this grower-owned organization had not only thrived to become a billion-dollar industry, but had built a trademark and licensing expertise that was opening unprecedented avenues of growth.

Hanlin shook his head, thinking back to the quiet citrus groves of California and Arizona. Not bad, he thought, not bad at all for a company built on a gift from Nature and the desperate dreams of a hundred California orange growers facing ruin over a century before.

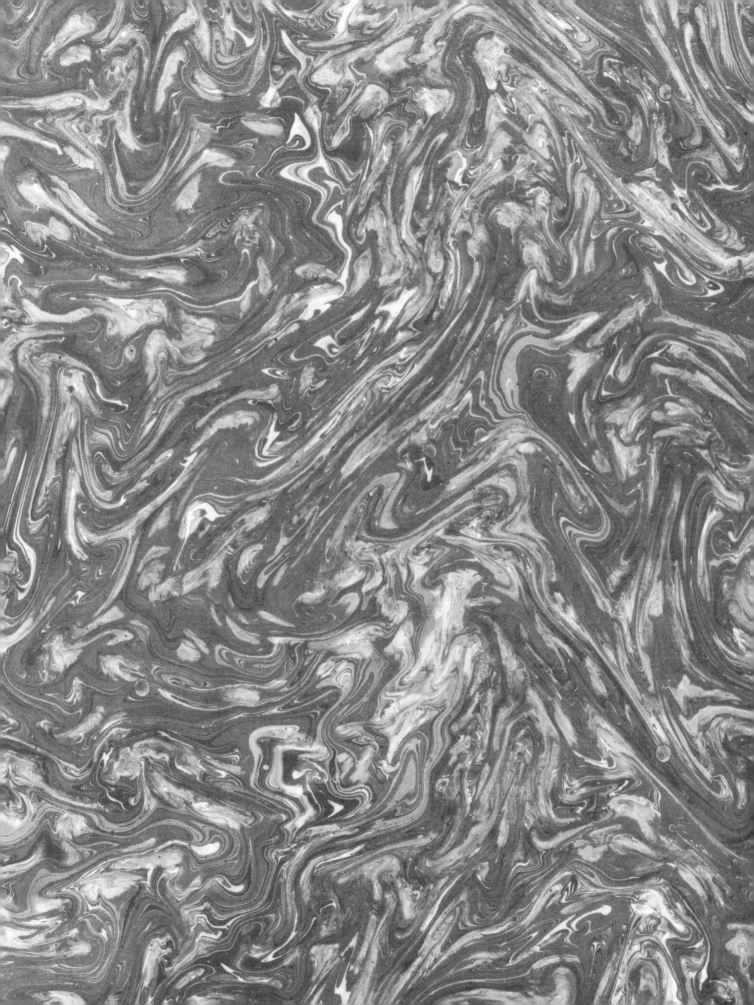

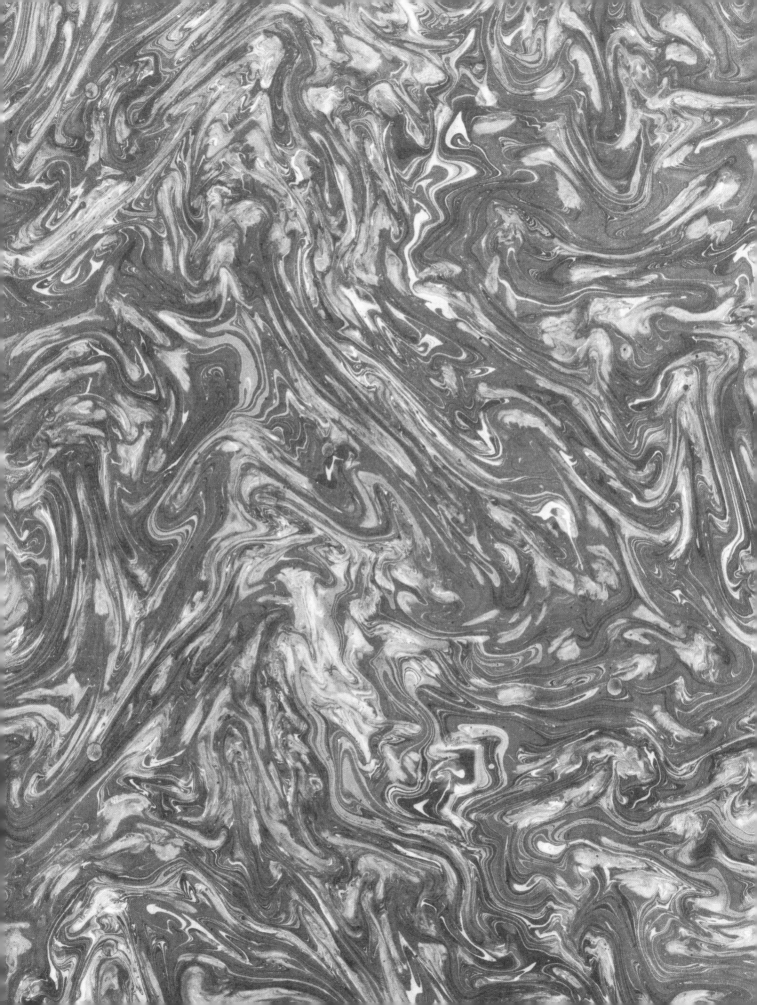

CHAPTER I – 1769 - 1893

CITRUS COMES TO CALIFORNIA

San Gabriel Mission, from an engraving appearing in the Semi Tropic California of June, 1881.

Modern California is a place of contradictions and extremes, at once America's richest agricultural producer and the most populous state in the country, the center of new trends, gleaming automobiles, and big dreams.

California is the story of land and people. You could chart the course of California history by studying the change in property values and population figures over the years. In 1920, you could buy an acre of Ventura County citrus land for $175; today, you could easily pay $25,000 for that same piece of property. In 1990, California was home to more people than any other state in America, with 30 million residents. In 1845, there were only 7,000 people here, not counting full-blooded Indian natives. The dramatic changes in land and people not only shaped the California of 1993, but left it a startlingly different place from what it was in the 19th century.

CITRUS COMES TO CALIFORNIA

Still governed by Spain, "Alta" California was, in the 1800s, a sleepy, pastoral land of pueblos and presidios, ranchos and missions. Spanish padres, inspired by the gentle climate, had founded a string of adobe missions, the first in San Diego in 1769. Those hardy missionaries brought with them the seeds for the first citrus fruit California would know. It was at one of these missions – San Gabriel near Los Angeles – that the first California orchard of any real size was planted about 1804.

Around 1840, with the region now under the influence of Mexican governors, California's first commercial orchard was planted by William Wolfskill in what is now downtown Los Angeles. These trees, as were all of California's early orange groves, were grown from seed.

The orange production's start was timely, for shortly after, citrus would see a boom of sorts with California's "Gold Rush." The heavy influx of fortune seekers following the discovery of gold in 1848 found California unprepared for their food requirements. Lacking vitamin-rich fruits and vegetables, many developed scurvy. As word spread that citrus could prevent the disease, demand skyrocketed. Soon, lemons were selling for $1 each, and lemon juice at a hefty $1 an ounce.

CALIFORNIA'S "VERITABLE" CITRUS BOOM

But the real boom for California's citrus industry occurred around the 1870s. It started with the completion of the transcontinental railroad, with its famous meeting-point ceremony at Promontory, Utah in 1869.

The citrus boom took another step in the 1870s with the introduction of the sweet, seedless navel orange. Sent from Brazil by American missionaries, this orange was first called the "Riverside navel" and later named the "Washington navel."

The navel adapted well to California. A family named Tibbets planted the first two navel trees in what is now the heart of the city of Riverside. In 1875, they picked California's first navel orange from the two trees that were to become famous. Neighbors who had been content with haphazard seedling fruit were amazed at this seedless fruit with its beautiful color and flavor. Immediately, the grafting of budwood was started from those two trees, and the Tibbets were soon doing a good business selling buds at $5 each to other growers.

California's citrus industry also advanced during this time with the realization that oranges would grow better away from the foggy coastline. It was learned that the winter-ripening navels favored the Riverside area. Valencias, "the summer orange," thrived in Orange County. Ventura, San Diego and Santa Barbara counties produced the finest lemons.

And also contributing to the citrus boom was the "health rush" to Southern California. The state's climate and year-round sunshine were used to lure Easterners out West for health reasons. Playing a lead role in this California promotion was the Southern Pacific Railway, eager to sell its vast amounts of land and to ship agricultural products East. It played on the appeal of scented orange blossoms and the promise of glorified farming to draw people to Southern California.

California saw the impact of the transcontinental railroad work both ways. It not only brought in hungry, ambitious farmers and immigrants from the East, but also allowed shipments from the West easier access to East Coast markets. With that opportunity, citrus growers expanded their acreage. Within ten years of the first rail shipment, the volume of California citrus moving East had grown to more than 2,000 cars annually. In another five years, it had doubled – and this at a time when oranges were considered a luxury, to be bought by the rich alone or only on festive occasions.

"It was not until the opening of the Atchison, Topeka and Santa Fe (rail) lines in 1885 that the highest development took place," Rahno Mabel MacCurdy wrote in *The History of the California Fruit Growers Exchange* (now Sunkist) in 1925. With a railroad extending into Los Angeles, Southern California now had a line of communication with the East.

"From this time on there was a veritable boom in orange planting," MacCurdy noted. "Some of the returns from these orchards were almost incredible, as much as $3,000 from one acre having been reported, and $800 to $1,000 being no uncommon yield. Of course, an industry that would pay such profits was eagerly sought. . . . The very face of Nature was changed, and in a few years Southern California became one of the most important sections of the state."

In 1887, the ventilated freight car was developed, followed two years later by the ice-bunker car. Both helped reduce decay in transit, and helped increase rail shipments of citrus.

Helped by the railroad, the navel orange and the lemon gave California a badly needed economic boost. For years, the fruit was one of the state's few exportable commodi-

One of the two original navel trees planted by Eliza and Luther Tibbets in 1873 in their yard in Riverside. Replanted in Riverside's Mission Inn Courtyard in 1903 by President Theodore Roosevelt, this tree died in 1921. The other parent tree thrives in Riverside and still produces fruit.   Inset: Mrs. Eliza Tibbets, a Riverside pioneer, is credited with planting California's first two Washington navel orange trees in 1873. Sent from Brazil, the seedlings were planted in the Tibbets' yard in Riverside, and given great care by Mrs. Tibbets and her husband Luther. Their sweet, seedless oranges created a sensation and helped launch Southern California's modern citrus industry.

ties, and the revenues it reaped from Eastern and Midwestern markets helped finance California's early growth. Counties like Riverside, Orange, San Diego, Ventura and Santa Barbara flourished as a result of the citrus industry. The city of Los Angeles increased from just over 11,000 people in 1880 to over 50,000 just 10 years later. Citrus communities like Pasadena, Riverside, San Bernardino, Anaheim, and Orange prospered. Between 1880 and 1893, California's citrus acreage jumped from 3,000 to over 40,000. Paralleling its citrus expansion, California gained almost 350,000 in population to reach 1.2 million people between 1880 and 1890.

"RUIN STARED HIM IN THE FACE"

But the rewards earned from the sales of California's citrus did not always extend to the growers out in the orange groves.

During the earlier days of California's citrus industry, growers had not fared too badly. Shipping agents handled all picking, packing and marketing details on an outright sale basis. An agent would visit the grove, estimate the value of the fruit on the tree, and strike a bargain with the grower. From that point on, the fruit was the agent's property and responsibility.

This seemed to work reasonably well – for a while. But by the mid-1880s, Southern California's citrus production was far above what local markets could handle. Despite the advent of the railroad, California growers' biggest market had remained local consumers.

California's citrus growers began to realize their survival depended on moving their fruit to distant markets. They were, however, faced with the reality of weak distribution methods. Agents in California were dispatching fruit with no knowledge of what was happening at its destination. They had no idea how much fruit competitors were moving. Some markets were glutted while others got nothing at all. With refrigeration still far from being perfected, fruit deteriorated en route.

Then, in 1891, the citrus marketing system took on a new twist. Seeing the predicament caused by the distribution methods, agents decided they would no longer buy fruit F.O.B. *(Freight-on-board: a purchase term meaning the buyer pays the transportation charges and assumes all risk of damage and delay in transit not caused by the shipper.)* Instead, the agents decided they would handle the citrus only on consignment, where fruit was shipped off and payment made only if a sale was made. That shifted the risk from distributor to grower. Now, when the farmer's crop left the orchard, he would have no guarantee of a sale.

Agents continued to supervise the movement of fruit from orchards to wholesale markets but now the growers bore full financial responsibility. Already challenged by Mother Nature, growers had to hope no freeze or heat wave would destroy their chances. If they were lucky enough to produce good fruit, they still had to pay their agents for pick-

These well-tended citrus groves belonged to E.H. Workman, at one time park commissioner of Los Angeles. This 1869 photo shows Workman's holdings, consisting of one block bounded by Main, Hill, Tenth, and Eleventh Streets in Los Angeles. The view is looking north from Eleventh Street.

The First Special Orange Train – The first shipment loaded exclusively with oranges leaves Los Angeles' River Station February 14, 1886. Traveling via the Southern Pacific and Union Pacific Railways, the shipment headed East to the Missouri River on express train time. This view is looking southwest. The building on the left is the ticket office and hotel; on the right is the freight depot. River Station was the city's only railroad depot at that time.

Huge blocks of ice helped rail cars keep citrus shipments from decaying as they headed East in the late 1880s and early 1890s. Though far from perfect, ice-bunker cars helped increase the volume of citrus shipments.

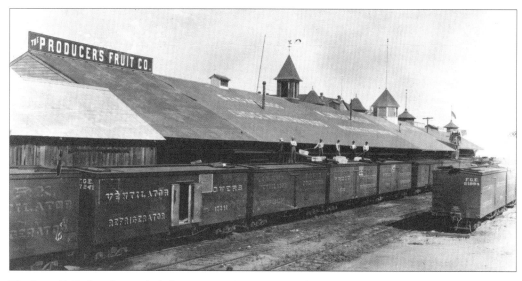

The Santa Fe Railroad extended a line into Los Angeles in 1885, adding to the already-existing Southern Pacific rail line. With two lines of communication with the East, the state's population boomed. Competing to bring in newcomers from the East, the two railroads engaged in a rate war, with the price of a ticket from Kansas City to Los Angeles dropping at one point to $1.

Early 1900s – early citrus shipments of the Southern California Fruit Exchange, now known as Sunkist Growers.

ing, freight and marketing, whether or not that fruit ever sold. In those consignment days, a grower could receive nothing for his fruit and still have to pay his agent a handling charge of 50 cents a box.

Years later, William Prior Russell, an orange grower in the 1880s, explained in a letter to MacCurdy how the system enabled citrus buyers to reject any amount they wished since they were the judges of what was marketable.

"I remember one year in the late Eighties," Russell wrote, "I sold my crop to [a citrus buyer]. He was to pay me one and three-fourths cents per pound, delivered to his packing-house. After delivering three or four loads, I asked to be shown how they had graded out, and found they had thrown out fifty percent as unmerchantable. . . . I insisted that I be allowed to take my discarded oranges home – hired a small grader, engaged a good packer. I graded the fruit and nailed the boxes myself and shipped them local freight. . . to San Francisco, and got a better net price for the discarded oranges than [the citrus buyer] paid me."

Desperate to receive a payback, many growers often shipped recklessly, demoralizing markets. Inadequate transportation facilities led to decay of fruit in transit. It was free-for-all for speculators. Farmers found themselves in weak bargaining positions, forced either to accept whatever might be offered them by local speculators or consign their fruit to the commission men in the East. "Either way, ruin stared him in the face," MacCurdy wrote in *The History of the California Fruit Growers Exchange.*

The whole scenario created a series of disastrous seasons called the "red ink" years, reportedly because growers' account sales were made out in red ink to reflect their losses. This period saw growers' sales often net less than packing, transportation and marketing expenses. Sometimes fruit fell to the ground to rot because oranges were bringing such low prices it did not pay to produce them. Orange grower William Russell later remembered, "About 1890, I could not sell at any price."

Across the U.S., similar troubles were leading the country as a whole towards the Great Depression of the early 1890s. For California's individual citrus growers in particular, it was a bleak time. Although citrus comprised 40,000 acres at that time, making it the state's second largest crop, the future of Southern California's citrus industry looked dubious.

DESPERATE EFFORTS

Tired of disastrous prices and what MacCurdy referred to as "the apparent dishonesty" of many commission houses in handling the orange crop of Southern California, growers began discussing ways to solve their difficulties. It was obvious they would have to find better distribution methods for their crop. And it was becoming increasingly clear that the

Chamber of Commerce rooms were housed in this livery building at First and Broadway streets in Los Angeles. On April 4, 1893, Southern California citrus leaders, including T.H.B. Chamblin, W.A. Spaulding, P.J. Dreher, and W.M. McFadden, assembled here in a "pre-Exchange meeting" to discuss organizing a region-wide citrus growers' marketing organization.

answer lay in taking charge of their own industry, with marketing experts who had the growers' interests at heart.

Growers began meeting in churches and Chamber of Commerce halls across Southern California's citrus belt, discussing ways to extricate themselves from their dismal position.

"At a meeting of growers held in Los Angeles October 24, 1885, the delegates by formal resolution recognized the fact that unless some united action was taken for improved methods in the sale of their fruit, they would soon lose their homes," MacCurdy wrote.

Meeting day and night for several days during the fall of 1885, the growers finally created The Orange Growers Protective Union of Southern California, their first attempt at uniting to market fruit. According to MacCurdy, it was J. Debarth Shorb of San Gabriel who took the initiative in organizing the Union. The Union – "one of growers and for the interests of growers" – sent salaried employees to Eastern markets to choose "reliable commission men" to oversee distribution of members' fruit. An attempt was made to regulate the shipments so that no market would be overstocked. In fact, it was recorded that "the cornerstone of this Union is intelligent distribution." But the Union lacked organization and coordination. This, and persistent opposition by commission men and buyers, led to the demise of the organization after a few years.

About the same time, three other organizations attempted to coordinate grower and packer interests: Fruit Growers Union of Southern California (1891), Riverside Orange Trust (1891), and Riverside Orange Growers and Packers Protection Association (1892-93). This last venture tried to represent both growers and packers. After operating for a short time, and none too smoothly due to internal friction as well as outside opposition, the Riverside Association failed, as the other two attempts had already done.

Yet all these attempts set the stage for the eventual cooperative that was to succeed so phenomenally. Something of the self-help spirit of those first attempts refused to die. It may have been the desperation of growers as they tried to find a way to solve their marketing dilemma, or their unwillingness to give up.

California growers were not alone in their troubles. In 1893, farmers across the U.S. were experiencing difficult times, with poor prices and weak bargaining positions. Despite the new telegraph invention, California's citrus farmers faced problems made worse by the distance of 2,000-3,000 miles that separated them from Eastern markets. In California's citrus groves, middlemen were telling growers how to pick their fruit, what qualities and grades they would handle, and allegedly even districting the orange-producing territory among themselves. In 1893, U.S. President Grover Cleveland may not have been aware of it, but most California orange growers were facing impending calamity.

PACKING LABELS: A UNIQUE LOOK INTO CALIFORNIA HISTORY

When citrus growers first began to identify their fruit, it is said they simply sten-ciled their names on the heads of their wooden citrus crates. Commercial adver-tising soon entered the picture and an art form developed that was uniquely Southern Californian.

Late in the 19th century, the first paper labels were attached to the citrus crates. These first labels were small circles of paper, about six inches in diameter, which were placed in the center of the stenciled design. Soon larger, rectangular labels, about 11 inches by 10 inches in size, replaced the stencil and round paper label.

In time, millions of the colorful paper labels were used by California citrus growers to identify and advertise the wooden boxes of fruit they shipped throughout the United States. The brightly colored labels became a means of dis-tinguishing one packer's shipment from his neighbors'. They were also a mark of a grower's success.

Each packinghouse had its own brands according to the grade of the fruit. The top grade bore its own name and the lesser grades possessed other labels. The brands were printed on colorful paper labels which were pasted on the ends of the fruit boxes.

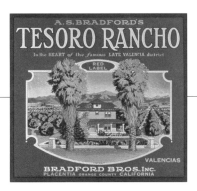

These labels had names like "Blue Top," "Highbrow," "Hollywood," "Clare-mont Gold," "Shining Star," and "Warrior."

The commercial artists who created the labels not only captured the spirit of the times, but the surroundings of Southern California in their artworks. In fact, one of the most important applications of box label art was in the "selling" of California. It is now possible to identify many landscapes, towns and groves from their representations on the citrus labels. As a result, the labels offer a unique look into the history of California.

Three different forms evolved over the 70-year period in which citrus labels were born. From 1885-1920, the labels evoked scenes of naturalism. Advertising dominated the look of the labels from 1920-1935. And from 1935-1955, the labels took on a commercial art form. Throughout the 70-year era of citrus labels, it is said that over 8,000 distinct designs were developed and used on over 2 billion boxes of oranges.

As the traditional wood box made way for the pre-printed cardboard carton in the 1950s, this unique art form was phased out.

Yet citrus crate art has survived to become a highly collectible item of paper Americana. Labels which were once hauled to the dump and burned now command prices as high as $100 each. Interestingly, other fruit and vegetable labels of the same period have not developed a following equal to that of citrus labels.

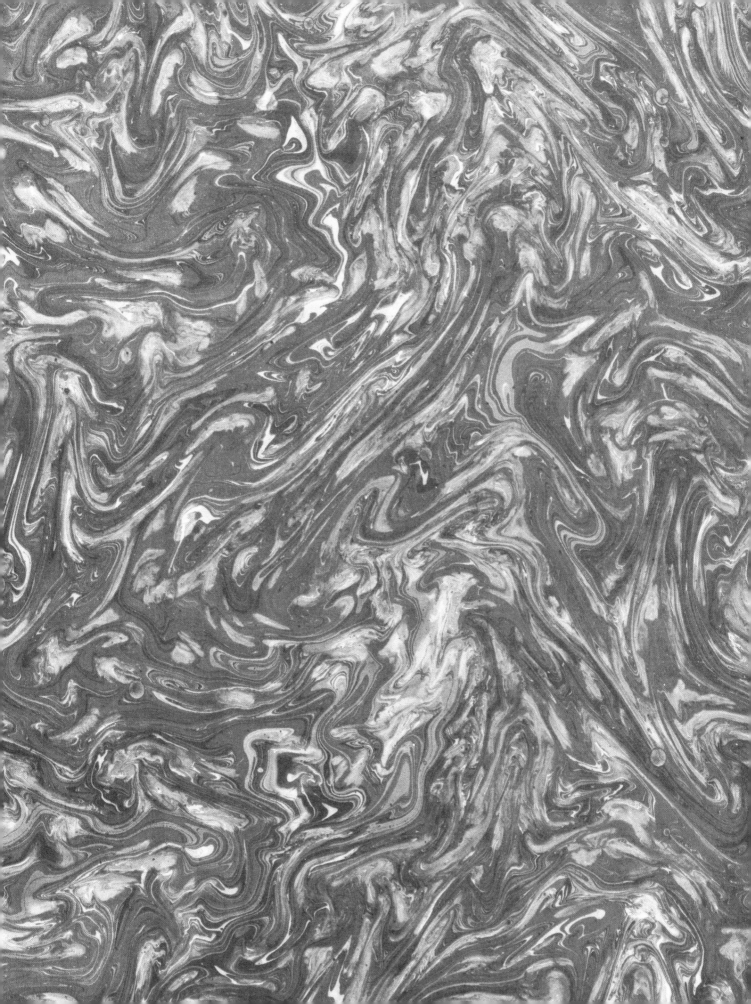

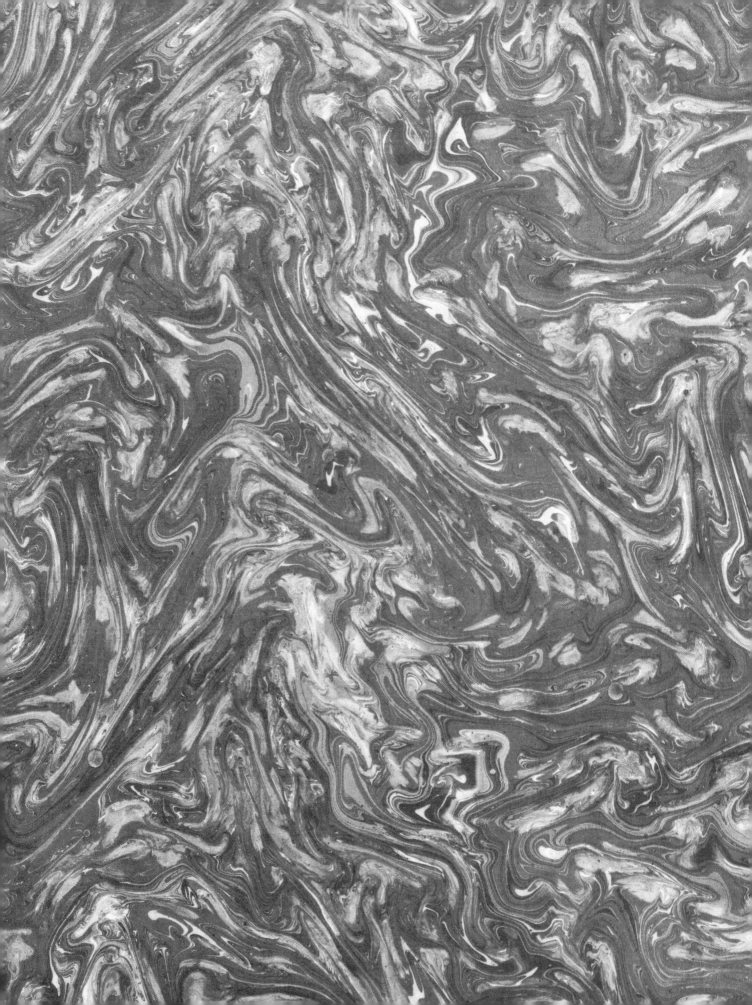

CHAPTER II – 1893 - 1903

THE FIRST STEPS

T.H.B. Chamblin, "the pioneer of the cooperative movement in California." The Pachappa Orange Growers Association he founded near Riverside in 1892 helped lay the foundation for the Sunkist organization.

Riverside's A.H. Naftzger served as President of the Southern California Fruit Exchange from 1894 - 1904, and was the first to bear the title of "General Manager."

QUIETLY SUCCESSFUL PIONEERS: CLAREMONT AND PACHAPPA

While most orange growers were struggling to stay in business, two small citrus associations in Southern California had quietly – and almost simultaneously – found ways to profitably market their fruit.

One was the Claremont Fruit Growers Association, which had operated under president P.J. Dreher in the upper Pomona Valley since 1892.

The Danish-born Dreher had come to California around 1885 in poor health. In fact, Ed Ainsworth's *Journey With The Sun,* written in 1968, reported that Dreher had suffered a breakdown in 1884 in Illinois and was given six weeks to live. "He came to California in a desperate effort to recuperate, and felt so much better that he brought his family out, and bought 40 acres of citrus land near Claremont," Ainsworth wrote.

The Claremont association had broken away from the system of non-grower shippers and packers, and was governed by growers themselves. Marketing directly through agents in the East, Claremont put great emphasis upon quality. Its top grade "Indian Hill" brand was the California citrus industry's first copyrighted label. And against a background of practically industrywide loss, Claremont had earned its growers $1.32 per box by the spring of 1893. The association would even take an aggressive step with a unique experiment. In April 1893, it sent a shipment of its top-quality Indian Hill oranges to England. The oranges arrived a month later, delighting Queen Victoria with their "handsome appearance and flavor," the *Pomona Weekly Times* reported.

The other grower marketing group, Pachappa Orange Growers Association in Riverside, also had been in operation since 1892. Operating under the cooperative tenet of banding together and selling their fruit by a pooling system, Pachappa had begun with just 11 neighbors and friends who grew citrus.

Headed by grower T.H.B. Chamblin, the Pachappa organization also differed in crucial ways from the previous grower marketing attempts. Growers signed a contract to deliver all of their fruit through one packinghouse, not just wherever they could get the best deal. This gave the group unity and strength. The Pachappa group, which included A.H. Naftzger and M.J. Daniels, could see that it would have a stronger foundation if it handled every process from the grove to the wholesaler, including picking and packing.

Pachappa employed no agents in Eastern markets but made arrangements with wholesalers by mail and shipped fruit to them on F.O.B. terms. Members were required to pay their fair proportion of the association's general expenses for packing and marketing. Any grower causing detriment to the association, such as delivering poor quality fruit, could be excluded from its operations. Each grower would receive his pro rata share of the net proceeds of the fruit that was sold and shipped. And each grower would be compensated according to the quality of his own fruit.

CLAREMONT'S SHIPMENT TO QUEEN VICTORIA

"In April, 1893, a carload of choice oranges was shipped to England via the Santa Fe by the Claremont Fruit Growers Association. Perfect and large, each piece of fruit was packed with the utmost care. One box was consigned to Queen Victoria with the compliments of the Association. Each box of the shipment held a letter, enclosed in an envelope, on the neat lithographed heading of the association. The letter read:

Claremont, California, U.S.A. April 14, 1893

To the Consumer and Dealer in England:
    These oranges were cut from the trees April 8 and packed and shipped this day over the Santa Fe route fast freight line to New York, there to take the fast steamer for Liverpool, England. This is the initial shipment by this Association to England of their Seedless Washington Navel Oranges, and it is made in an experimental way to test the carrying and keeping qualities of our fruits, which we believe to be the very best. We would be pleased to have you report to us their quality, flavor and condition. Believing they will meet such reception and appreciation as to merit our further shipments, we most respectfully commend them to lovers of choice fruits.

    The letter is said to have been the first attempt to advertise California oranges."

- *The Sunkist Courier,* 1935

18

Pachappa was operating as a true cooperative, and it was working, something outside citrus growers could not ignore. In the spring of 1893, the association returned $1.00 per box to members while outside growers received 30 to 50 cents. Immediately, several prominent orange growers and businessmen approached the Pachappa group to learn more about its success.

Today, Pachappa's Chamblin is called the pioneer of the cooperative movement in California. But in 1893, he was simply an Ohio-born man nearly 60 years old who, as MacCurdy recorded, used "earnest, forcible, convincing arguments presented in a clear, concise manner that appealed to the common sense of growers."

According to Ainsworth's *Journey With The Sun,* Chamblin had left the Midwest as a newspaper publisher, coming to California around 1880 to find a cure for ill health. He had purchased an orange grove in Riverside, and struggled for several years with production and marketing problems. In fact, Ainsworth wrote, "Chamblin, like all the other growers, was so immersed for a while in his own back-breaking labors to avert financial ruin that he had little time to think about others."

Chamblin's experience with the Pachappa Orange Growers Association had given him the opportunity to familiarize himself with the methods of citrus marketing. Watching the troubles of Southern California's citrus growers, Chamblin had formulated a plan he felt would benefit them.

CHAMBLIN AND DREHER PRESENT THEIR PLANS

For weeks during early 1893, citrus growers around Southern California had been meeting in their local communities, trying to find a solution to their marketing dilemma. Having heard about the Pachappa and Claremont associations, they wanted to explore similar plans of organizing. Southern California's citrus marketing conditions had deteriorated so drastically, many felt any plan would be an improvement over what they were living with.

Yet there had been arguments about where these various growers should meet. Los Angeles had been suggested but some felt the city was too far from the citrus producing areas. It would cost many growers $3.50 just to get into the city.

Others felt there was too much jealousy between the various regions to hold an important meeting in one of the citrus producing communities. According to the March 22, 1893 issue of *The Los Angeles Times,* arguing at a meeting in Colton the week before had been getting out of control until Chamblin, who was present, stood up and said it mattered little where the meeting was held. The vital question, he said, was not the growing of oranges but the marketing of them. Applause was reported. Chamblin also urged the growers to lay their differences aside. And finally he said that it would be better to hold the first industry-wide meeting at a large commercial center like Los Angeles, and local meetings could be held afterwards. Again applause was heard.

On April 4, 1893, a group of about 100 prominent orange growers met in the Chamber of Commerce Hall on the second floor of the Mott building on Main Street in Los Angeles. They had come to hear Chamblin's plan for a general organization of local associations into a united front of Southern California orange growers. The attendees had names like W.A. Spaulding, W.E. Collins, E.W. Holmes, G.J. Griffith, W.M. McFadden, J.D. Reymert, and D. Hyer. Also present was Claremont's Dreher, then in his early 40s.

Chamblin presented his plan, based on his Riverside association. According to *The Los Angeles Times,* Chamblin said, "Among things which are absolutely essential to success are: Full provision for every grower; the marketing of each crop in proportion and at equal prices and the giving of each grower the full average of the market from the beginning of the season until the close.

"These things can be done," Chamblin insisted. "All that is required is the consent of the growers. . . . Let us have harmony. Let us forget which localities from which we come. Why is the market demoralized? It is from lack of method and system. Method and system contribute to success in all branches of business. The orange industry in Southern California has been left to drift. It is drifting away."

The group also heard from Claremont's Dreher, who spoke of his association's method of direct marketing to Eastern markets.

The reaction to Chamblin and Dreher that April day was immediate. Chamblin's plan not only drew applause but was "heartily received and endorsed," according to Mac-Curdy, as was Dreher's direct marketing method.

But implementing their ideas, those at the meeting realized, would require the hearty cooperation of every grower in the region. There was a general feeling from the leaders that unless 90 percent of the growers joined in the movement, there was little or no use in trying to do anything. In fact, Chamblin thought that if even 10 percent of the growers did not come into the movement, they could demoralize the market.

Chamblin knew there were many elements to harmonize. It would not do to wait until the harvest would begin. *The Los Angeles Times* reported what the general feeling was. "They (the leaders) must open the campaign in the spring and settle the question once and for all, or the citrus industry must go down," the newspaper observed. "They must burn it into the heart of every business man that on this question his prosperity depends."

As the historic meeting closed that April day in 1893, attention was called to the necessity of disseminating full information across Southern California about the objects of a unified marketing association. Growers would have to be educated gradually, so that all would understand and be able to explain it to others. The group formed a study committee to look into the logistics of the plan.

The five-member committee, headed by Dreher, met in Pomona. Years later, in 1943, as it remembered the cooperative's 50-year-old beginnings, *The Sunkist Courier* reported

Sunkist's second home was a suite of offices over a Riverside drugstore from 1893-94.

The early 1900s saw a surge of packinghouse renovation and modernization. It was during this decade that most packinghouses – like this one in the Claremont district – first hooked up to power that carried fruit along conveyer belts for sizing, washing, waxing, and grading.

that only one of these men was a rancher by profession; the other four were either retired or active in medicine or law. But bonded by a common interest in the future of the state's citrus industry, the men pooled their combined knowledge and experience. Within days, the committee had hammered out an outlay of plans for grower consideration based on the Pachappa and Claremont associations.

Returning to the Chamber of Commerce building in Los Angeles on May 9, the group recommended that nine districts be formed. They were:

Riverside County
All of San Bernardino east of Cucamonga
Cucamonga, Ontario, Pomona, Claremont, and San Dimas
That portion of Los Angeles County north of the Santa Fe Railroad and
east of the Los Angeles River
The remainder of Los Angeles County
Orange County
San Diego County
Ventura County
Santa Barbara County

Within each district, local associations would be organized to pack the fruit. Each association would establish a purely local brand without individual or company name attached. Each packer was to confine itself exclusively to the packing of association fruit. Fruit picking was pro-rated among grower-members who all would have an equal chance for delivery. They would share and share alike. Sales orders for fruit were likewise pro-rated among associations to keep fruit moving proportionately. To ensure quality, poor fruit would not be allowed to pool with fine fruit.

The committee also proposed that a central business office be established in each district, and kept open to all managers of associations in the district for handling telegrams and correspondence. Also recommended was a Southern California executive committee consisting of one member from each district to handle matters affecting all districts.

THE RIVERSIDE EXCHANGE FORMS -
"WE HAVE THE GOODS AND THE WORLD WANTS THEM"

Through the spring of 1893, word spread of this new kind of citrus marketing, one organized by and for growers. By May, the first exchange was formed under the guiding hand of Chamblin. Known as the "Riverside Fruit Exchange," the organization had a board of directors which met May 13 to discuss and explain its fundamental attitude and objectives.

In its meeting minutes, the board stated that the Riverside Fruit Exchange was not there to fix prices but to promote stability and permanence for Southern California's citrus industry. It sought to promote uniform and better methods of packing and handling. No longer would fruit go out on consignment, leaving growers empty-handed. Instead, payment advances would be made through arrangements with local banks. The collateral would be the crop, only now the security was in the hands of local associations, not in the hands of the consignee.

The Riverside Fruit Exchange also stressed it did not seek to make war on brokers and packers. But the dangers of haphazard marketing or unscrupulous middlemen had to be stopped if the industry was to endure.

"In this undertaking to protect ourselves," the board warned, "we shall expect to be threatened; every plausible argument and cunning device will be employed to break us into fragments. . . . The men who have grown rich from commissions and percentages will not abandon the field without a struggle.

"We are to seek not only to offer our goods in such attractive condition as to increase the demand and open new markets, but to so distribute so that every market shall be supplied and none glutted.

"In the production of good fruit, Southern California has passed the experimental stage. We have the goods and the world wants them. It is to be hoped that we are able to bring to the business such intelligence and capacity that from the point of production through to the point of consumption every detail shall show care, method and economy, that producer and consumer shall be mutually contented."

The board, which agreed to serve without compensation, also urged widespread support from growers. "We cannot succeed with a fragment of the crop; we need the aid of every grower."

"WHOLLY ON MY OWN ACCOUNT AND AT MY OWN RISK"

As the "Riverside" plan became known during that spring and summer of 1893, appeals for help began to come from all parts of Southern California's citrus belt. Almost immediately, plans were made to cover these other areas.

Chamblin and Dreher set out to explain the rudiments of the new cooperative plan. Ainsworth wrote that Chamblin had already begun to travel around the area with his new cooperative idea. Now, traveling by buggy or train, the two men journeyed extensively throughout Southern California to meet with growers. They were different in personality – Chamblin the persuasive, patient one; Dreher eager for direct action, impatient with delay and procrastination.

The campaign wasn't easy for either man. Each faced doubt, lethargy, hostility, even active opposition by commission agents, who spread the word that the citrus cooperative movement was "a flash in the pan." For some growers, caught in the depths of financial depression, the thought of releasing their money into an untried program was out of the question.

24

B.A. Woodford was the first manager of the Lemon Growers Exchange of Ontario and served as president of the Southern California Fruit Exchange from 1904-1912.

G. Harold Powell, a former U.S. Department of Agriculture official whose investigation into the causes of fruit decay led to radical changes in fruit handling, was general manager of the California Fruit Growers Exchange from 1912-1922.

P.J. Dreher, who headed Claremont Fruit Growers Association, one of the two early cooperative organizations that were forerunners of the Southern California Fruit Exchange, served as the Exchange president in 1920.

For Chamblin, who still wrestled with ill health, the call to citrus growers had become a crusade, not for personal gain but because he believed in the fundamental truths under which his Pachappa group had so successfully operated. "I was besieged with calls from other localities to extend the work," Chamblin would later say. "I hesitated because of ill health. Finally, under increased pressure, I consented. . . . Before beginning the work, I was urged to name the conditions, which I did as follows: I would make the campaign wholly on my own account and at my own risk. If I failed it would be my own failure, if otherwise, the orange growers would determine the matter of compensation."

Through those hot summer months of 1893, Chamblin continued to make his rounds. His theme to growers was, "Stand together or hang separately." As he traveled around the region, he met several influential men who would later become the leadership of the new cooperative organization. And with his newspaper background, Chamblin was able to gain favorable press for the citrus growers' movement.

Finally, with the word spread throughout the region, a meeting was called. On August 29, 1893, delegates of several local associations met in the assembly room of the Los Angeles Chamber of Commerce, just a few blocks from where William Wolfskill had planted California's first commercial orange grove back in 1840. Gathering as one central body, they discussed how region-wide organization and marketing would work under the new Riverside plan.

Because of the previous work done by Chamblin, Dreher and their colleagues, the associations and exchanges were already basically organized in every part of Southern California. The way was paved to unite.

THE SOUTHERN CALIFORNIA FRUIT EXCHANGE IS BORN

A general design for merging all district exchanges and associations was accepted, and a board was appointed which would serve as a Board of Control or marketing department. Eventually it would be called the executive board of the Southern California Fruit Exchange. Its office was in Riverside. That August day in 1893, officers were elected, many of them men Chamblin had met as he traveled to build support earlier that summer. The executive board's first president was H.R. Smith of the Semi-Tropic Fruit Exchange. Other Executive Board members were A.H. Naftzger, Earl Van Luven, W.H. Young, E.C. Kimbell, A.H. Cargill, H.L. Story, and Frank Scoville.

By the fall of 1893, seven exchanges had been formally organized. The largest, far and away, was the Riverside Fruit Exchange (Naftzger). The other six were the Semi-Tropic Fruit Exchange of Los Angeles (Smith), San Bernardino County Fruit Exchange of Colton (Van Luven), Duarte Fruit Exchange of Duarte (Young), Orange County Fruit Exchange of Orange County (Cargill), San Diego County Fruit Exchange of San Diego (Story), and San

Birthplace of the Southern California Fruit Exchange (now Sunkist) in 1893 – the old Chamber of Commerce assembly room in the Mott Building on North Main Street near Market in downtown Los Angeles.

Antonio Fruit Exchange of Pomona (Kimbell). An eighth, the Queen Colony Fruit Exchange (Scoville), would be admitted to membership in October of 1894.

General manager of the Southern California Fruit Exchange was W.A. Perry of Riverside. In a flyer dated November 29, 1893, Perry announced that the fruit growers of Southern California had organized exchanges in the various districts for the purpose of "self protection," and that the movement was "assuming proportions of vast magnitude."

Set up as a federated structure, the Southern California Fruit Exchange was made up of regional marketing cooperatives – the district exchanges. This federation involved first a contractual relationship between the orange grower and his respective packinghouse association. The next step in the structure was the district exchange, which required at least three associations with the sum total of their products comprising at least 500 shipping carloads a season. (Three hundred boxes of fruit constituted a carload.) The exchanges were then represented in the cooperative's marketing efforts by the board of directors, or executive board. Each director had one vote.

One of the cornerstones of the new organization was quality. Growers and packing houses were required to discipline themselves to reach the highest grading standards for their fruit.

For a while, the executive board met at the offices of the Riverside Fruit Exchange in Riverside. But deciding a more central location was needed, it moved into new quarters March 1, 1894 at Spring and Franklin Streets in Los Angeles. Monthly rent for the office space was $12.50. E.C. Kimbell would serve as general manager, taking over from W.A. Perry, who had been serving in that role since August 1893. H.R. Smith would serve as president of the board until October 1894, when he would be succeeded by A.H. Naftzger.

The executive board made sure that markets were covered by brokers under the supervision of an Eastern representative with headquarters in Chicago. During the 1893-94 season, that representative was H.K. Pratt. Later, in 1894-95, P.E. Platt would represent the whole territory east of the Mississippi River.

During its first season, the Exchange represented a full 80 percent of the orange growers of Southern California, shipping 6,000 carloads of the state's 7,000 total. By regulating shipments and avoiding gluts, the Exchange surprised even its members with its returns. The average net price of all oranges marketed through the San Antonio Exchange brought growers about $1 per box. Many felt that had it not been for the association's marketing plan, the crop that year would not have netted even 25 cents per box. And, by watching costs and keeping expenses low, the Exchange had operated at an expense of only 1-1/2 cents per box. That compared to a 25-cent per-box commission growers would have had to pay commission agents.

The *Pomona Weekly Times,* which had been watching the growers' plan unfold, reported on the state of affairs during the summer of 1894, the end of the first season.

"The various orange growers' associations are closing up accounts of the first season's business," the newspaper reported. "Delayed accounts have prevented a final settlement in a few cases, but as far as finally closed, the wisdom of the association plan has been demonstrated. And it must be remembered that the season was unfavorable because of many frosted oranges, dull times east, strong opposition by the old shippers, lack of unanimity of action among the growers and inexperience, but with all these adverse influences the actual results ought to induce all growers to join the associations."

By December 1894, with Naftzger as president, the executive board of the Exchange reported that its eight exchanges handled four-fifths of Southern California's orange crop. In the fall of 1895, over twenty agents were appointed to attend exclusively to Exchange business in the East. In June 1895, A.W. Frost had been named temporarily as general manager. By December, A.H. Cargill had moved to the position.

The Exchange was making a successful start in both sales returns and in reductions of incidental costs. But growing pains were on the way, and the faith of its members was about to be tested.

GROWING PAINS, CONFUSION AND PROBLEMS

Over the first two seasons, the organization's share of Southern California oranges grew, reaching 80 percent by December, 1894, according to MacCurdy. Then, abruptly, its share plummeted to just 32 percent in the 1895-96 season. Returns, which had totaled just over $1 million in the 1895-96 season, plunged to $858,000 the next year. By 1896-97, the Exchange's share had dropped to 23 percent.

The sudden downturn surprised many. Had the Exchange grown too quickly, they wondered? Had their expectations been too high? Had officials devised a flawed system?

The truth lay mostly in inexperience. It wasn't that the men chosen to direct the new organization had anything but the best intentions. They were intelligent and honest. But they were unpracticed in the complex world of direct marketing. And charged with entrusting their neighbors' livelihoods, they were understandably timid. Many of the association and exchange managers also were inexperienced. The executive board was not always fully advised of shipments by exchanges so competition existed between Exchange fruit in Eastern markets.

And there was the strenuous opposition of established dealers, just as the growers' organizers had foreseen. Some of the old established dealers who had formerly been able to control the market for their own purposes now worked to disrupt the fledgling cooperative. Parties hostile to interests of the Exchange would intentionally glut markets in anticipation of the arrival of the cooperative's fruit.

Three years before, when the Exchange was being formed, growers had been determined not to repeat their earlier bad experiences with consignment sales. So they had insisted the new association make its sales on F.O.B. terms. Twice a month, F.O.B. orange prices were published by the Exchange for its members. While this avoided the middle-man in Eastern markets, it naturally left Exchange prices vulnerable. The result was that dealers outside the Exchange would lower non-member fruit to prices just under those of the cooperative.

Inexperience, competition, flawed business practices – all these were leading the Exchange down a path of failure. In the growing atmosphere of confusion and problems, growers began to give up their membership and turned to selling fruit outside the cooperative. Maybe the warning voices had been right; the new venture was a flash in the pan. Many growers bore no loyalty to the new cooperative. As an added problem, Exchange founders had failed to incorporate the organization, leaving it powerless to take action against growers who broke contracts with the new association.

Agents returned to the groves, wooing growers away from the Exchange with offers of higher prices. So high was the drop-out rate that, in the summer of 1895, the Exchange board temporarily disbanded. But unwilling to let the dream die, the directors re-grouped immediately. Within weeks, Chamblin, Naftzger and Dreher, among others, reinforced the Southern California Fruit Exchange.

RE-GROUPING

One major change Exchange directors made was to incorporate their organization. Better business methods were introduced to prevent gluts of fruit. More flexible sales procedures were implemented. Because the conditional terms of F.O.B. sales had cost the Exchange nearly $100,000 in rejected shipments in a single season, the board now adopted a plan for selling on a delivered price basis. Prices were no longer published. Selling agents were appointed to handle sales in Eastern markets. Uncertain growers were urged to stand firm in the belief that the cooperative would succeed.

In September 1896 – as the first automobiles were beginning to appear in Southern California – A.W. Frost was once again appointed general manager of the Exchange, but replaced in November by J.E. Packard.

Quantity of shipments and the percent of total industry crop the Exchange handled began to climb. It rose from 23 percent to 25 by the 1897-98 season. By 1897, with the dynamic A.H. Naftzger now serving as both president and general manager, the Exchange was supported by a network of 11 district exchanges and 37 associations. It maintained representatives in 70 cities throughout the East and Midwest. It opened a sales office in Buffalo, N.Y. to cover the territory of Erie, Pennsylvania, Toronto, Ontario, and all of upper New York state as far east as Albany. With salaried sales offices in the East, Exchange business in 1897-98 reached a record $1.67 million, shipping over 4,000 rail cars of citrus. By 1899, total sales of the Buffalo office alone amounted to 301 cars of citrus, a figure large enough to require hiring an additional employee at a salary of $5 a week. Much of the fruit also was sold at auctions in Eastern cities.

As the century closed, the Exchange began to stand on solid ground. Competition from commission agents was still powerful, but the Exchange managed to hold its own. Though it handled only 33 percent of California's citrus crop in the 1899-1900 season, the Exchange could boast 1,700 members from 75 local packing associations and 12 district exchanges. Its sales returns rose to almost $3.7 million that season from only $1.7 million the year before. All proceeds, minus the actual cost of doing business, were returned to members. And leaders like Chamblin waited patiently, certain that time would see the Exchange prevail.

LEMON GROWERS ORGANIZE: "A KNOCK-DOWN ARGUMENT"

"But what of lemons?" MacCurdy would ask in her 1925 history of the California Fruit Growers Exchange.

California's commercial lemon industry had been growing since it started around 1880 with the introduction of the Eureka and Lisbon lemon varieties. At about that time, growers had also discovered that, unlike oranges, the fruits could be picked while still green and held for an extended period in a cool dry place until they were properly cured.

While orange growers were struggling to band together, lemon producers were facing similar marketing troubles. California lemons were not only failing to capture Eastern markets, but were even competing in Los Angeles and San Francisco with lemons imported from the Mediterranean. Lemon growers had the same problems as orange producers with speculators and middlemen, and Eastern fruit merchants complained that California lemons were often not fresh when they arrived and were carelessly packed.

Growers were urged "to maintain an evenness of pack and to establish a brand that the trade respects, and one that buyers will endorse by purchasing by reason of its established reputation for reliableness," an I.C. Wood was quoted in the *Ontario Record* in October 1893.

Yet there were some exceptions. The citrus which California lemon pioneer Nathan W. Blanchard was shipping into Chicago in 1890 so pleased his buyer that the merchant declared, "I do not think that any better lemons grow on earth."

In the autumn of 1893, determined to establish a strong reputation in Eastern markets for the fine lemons which Southern California was capable of producing, several lemon growers from the Ontario and Cucamonga areas of Southern California met. Those present at the Magnolia Villa that October day included Messrs. J.W. Freeman, E.M. Hatch, Adams, Hyer, Woodford, C.E. Harwood of Ontario and G.R. Thayer of Cucamonga. All realized it was important to establish a good reputation for the lemon industry while it was still in its infancy.

From the beginning, the exchange was devoted to quality and consistency in its packing operations. Here, workers in the early 1900's are pictured sizing fruit.

Packing citrus in the early 1900s. Each piece of fruit was wrapped in tissue printed with the Sunkist name.

Out of that meeting, the Lemon Growers Exchange of Ontario was formed "to secure the uniform picking, grading, curing and packing of lemons and their most profitable marketing under a common brand." It was duly noted that the new organization would not antagonize the orange growers' new efforts but would work along the same lines. Five incorporators were elected: Hatch, Freeman, Harwood, W.M. Stroud and Thayer. Later, the five were voted to the association's board of directors, with Harwood as president. B.A. Woodford was named manager.

In forming the new lemon marketing cooperative, the growers decided that the success of their plan depended on having a single central curing house under one management. By December, the Exchange had adopted the "Sicily" box for packing, a size used by Florida packers and considered more acceptable to Eastern dealers than the ordinary California box. The new association approved three brands: the Bear, the Eagle and the Owl. "Each member of the association has a number which is marked on his boxes, and thus every individual's fruit is kept track of," the *Ontario Record* reported on December 13, 1893.

By January 1894, the Lemon Exchange was finding success. The returns from the first car of lemons shipped by the Exchange had netted members $2.60 per box of their first grade Bear brand lemons on F.O.B. terms. Second-grade Eagle brand had returned $2.10 per box and the third-grade Owl brand had brought in $1.85 per box.

"We know of no more forcible argument in favor of the Exchange and no more striking proof of its success than these figures," the *Ontario Record* reported on January 10, "and orders are rushing in faster than they can be filled."

And in what may have been the strongest testimony of all for the new grower-backed Lemon Exchange, the *Ontario Record* also noted, "The lemons which the Exchange is marketing as thirds and many of the seconds will not be handled at all by the commission men," who simply threw them out as culls.

"But the Exchange," the newspaper continued, "by careful grading and uniformity of curing, gets about $2.00 a box for this fruit that does not come up to the standard of first grade. This must be a kind of knock-down argument to any grower who has stayed out of the Exchange."

Through 1894, the reputation of the Lemon Exchange grew. That year, the *Ontario Record* would report that the association's pack had become "a favorite in some of the best markets."

Then, in the summer of 1895, talk surfaced of merging the orange growers' association with the lemon growers' efforts. The *Ontario Record* reported what some growers were saying. "No argument is now necessary to convince the orange growers of the advantage of cooperation in fruit marketing, but it will be clear to anyone who is familiar with the lemon business that there is even more need of unity of action with the lemon than with the orange," the newspaper observed. "There needs to be a nearly uniform system of curing and grading, and a plan which shall prevent undue competition with each other in the markets."

By November 1895, manager Woodford could report to members that their Lemon Growers Exchange had handled 1,709,175 pounds of the fruit that year. The cooperative had averaged a payment of $2.52 for every 100 pounds of lemons.

And in that same report, Woodford announced that the board of directors of the Lemon Growers Exchange had "seen fit to join the orange association in forming a district exchange (Ontario Fruit Exchange) which is a member of the Southern California Fruit Exchanges, and by this move they think you can more readily reach the Eastern markets and secure the best prices for your fruit."

So confident was the board of the ability of the Lemon Exchange to competitively market its fruit, several directors purchased fruit outright from some of the more independent lemon growers who refused to send their crop through cooperative channels. The directors sold the independents' lemons through the Exchange, earning prices so far above what outsiders had achieved that nearly every independent joined the Lemon Exchange. This swelled the volume, reduced the per capita cost and augmented the momentum of the new movement.

ORANGE AND LEMON GROWERS MERGE: "HARMONIZE, UNIFIED"

Ideas of merging the efforts of orange and lemon growers continued to escalate. In April 1896, a lemon growers' committee had been appointed to confer with the Southern California Fruit Exchange "to see what arrangements could be for the lemon growers to join said Exchange." As a result, MacCurdy wrote, the Exchange directors took action at their next meeting declaring "that it is the sense of this board that lemon growers or associations be admitted on the same basis as the orange and lemon growers have heretofore."

At a December 23, 1896 meeting, the lemon growers committee resolved that "the lemon interests can and should be harmonized with and unified in the Southern California Fruit Exchange by the recognition of an advisory board to be appointed by the lemon growing districts, which advisory board may recommend to the Southern California Fruit Exchange such methods pertaining to the lemon business as shall facilitate the handling of the fruit to the best advantage, even if necessary in the matter of the suggestion of lemon brokers. Said committee to work in harmony with the general plan of the Southern California Fruit Exchange." By 1897, orange and lemon growers were marketing their crops on the same basis through the regular Exchange departments. In the fall of 1897, Francis Q. Story, a Boston wool merchant turned California citrus grower, was elected president of the cooperative. Story would be unanimously elected president every year until 1920, when he chose to retire from the organization's top post.

F.Q. Story, Boston wool merchant turned California citrus grower, served as president of the Exchange from 1904-1920.

AUCTIONS: A VANISHED INDUSTRY TRADITION

They were called "the baseball cities" by Sunkist people, those towns in the eastern United States where auctions were once held to sell fresh fruit and vegetables. Held in cities known for their baseball teams – Chicago, Boston, Baltimore, Philadelphia, Pittsburgh, Cincinnati, Cleveland, St. Louis – auctions comprised an important sales outlet for the citrus industry from its earliest days.

The auctions drew buyers looking for fruit at bargain prices. Small grocery store owners, jobbers and wholesalers came regularly to buy whatever quantity of fruit they needed, whether it was five boxes or 100. Arriving as early as 3 o'clock in the morning, the buyers would inspect the lots of fruit on display which had arrived at the auction building by railcar hours before. Then, they would proceed to the auction room, where an auctioneer would direct the proceedings, using his gavel and the trade's own special vernacular to guide the frantic bidding on the fruit. Each lot of fruit had a number, which was used for bidding identification.

When the morning's auction was over, large amounts of money had traded hands. The buyers' trucks would carry the fruit home to its new destinations. By noon, the auction building was clean, silent and ready for the next day's business.

Sunkist representatives always participated in the auctions as one aspect of selling the cooperative's oranges and lemons. In fact, by the 1950s, one-fourth of Sunkist's fruit was sold at auction.

There were produce auctions in European cities, too. Some of the most prominent were in Rotterdam, Antwerp, Hamburg, and Le Havre, all operated much the same as America's fruit auctions. Japan operated an auction where bidding was conducted only with hand signals. Sunkist (then the California Fruit Growers Exchange) even ran its own auction in the early 20th century in Los Angeles. In addition to citrus, auctions offered produce such as pears, peaches, plums, and apples from California, Florida, and other areas.

Auctions began disappearing in the 1960s, casualties of the huge supermarkets which were appearing on the American scene. These large buying chains bought produce in mass quantities to distribute to their stores everywhere. The supermarkets required shipments as large as 50 carloads at a time, purchased in advance at firm prices so they could prepare their advertisements to consumers. The daily bidding battles and hectic atmosphere of the auctions could not meet those needs. By the 1970s, the auctions, a part of citrus industry tradition, were gone.

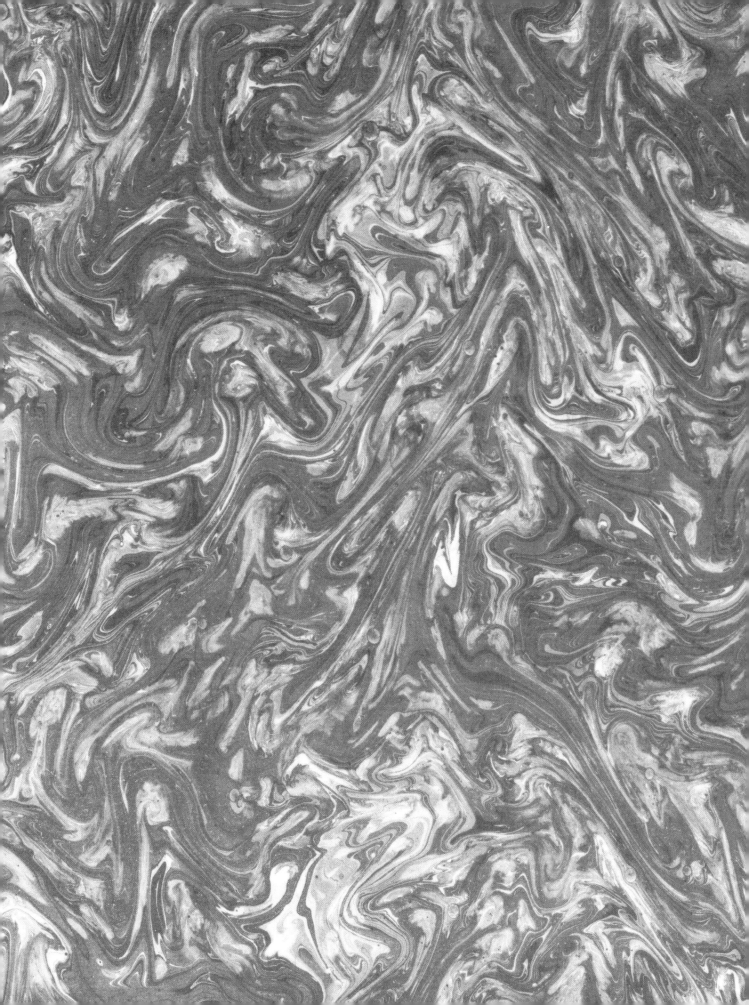

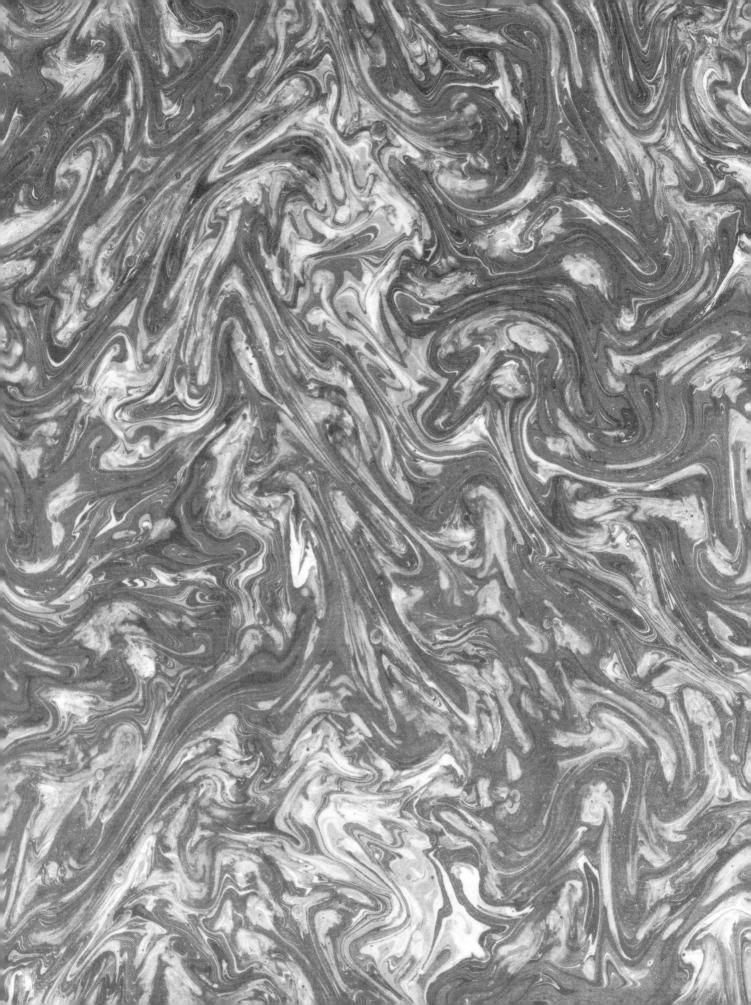

CHAPTER III – 1903 - 1920

BUILDING A NAME

President Theodore Roosevelt replants one of Eliza Tibbets' original navel trees in 1903 in the courtyard of Riverside's Mission Inn. The tree died in 1921. Inset: In 1916, the parent navel orange tree still thrived in the Mission Inn courtyard.

Ten years had passed since orange growers had formed the Southern California Fruit Exchange. Theodore Roosevelt now served as President of the United States. There were 45 states in the Union. America's population numbered over 76 million; California had about 1.5 million residents. The cooperative now represented 47 percent of the total output of oranges in the southern part of the state. But trouble lay ahead.

The 1902-03 season brought a large crop and intensified competition between the Exchange and independent shippers. In a plan designed to bring the divergent groups together and end the undercutting of prices, a new organization was formed on April 1, 1903. It was called the California Fruit Agency – a union of the Southern California Fruit Exchange and California Citrus Union, a group of independent shippers.

This venture was a break from the cooperative ideal of grower-owned marketing and control. Proponents, however, said the new agency promised a revolution in the methods previously used to market the citrus crops of Southern California. It would be to the "best advantage of all the growers." The new Agency would eliminate ruinous competition, prevent glutted markets, and provide equal distribution of output throughout the U.S., they said. Combining all the shippers would help secure a uniform price, protect the Eastern buyer and do away with heavy losses and hurtful speculation.

Some 90 percent of the growers and shippers joined the California Fruit Agency. But ultimately, the two groups were too far apart in their philosophies, and friction ensued. "It was like trying to mix oil and water," citrus grower C.C. Teague would later write. In fact, the huge Limoneira Ranch, which Teague managed, discontinued its membership during this time.

Added to the Agency's troubles was a subsequent year of poor returns. A severe, cold winter in the East hampered the peddling trade in some parts of the country, resulting in low prices for both Florida and California oranges.

Marketing conditions worsened until the Exchange was threatened with disruption. Finally, on May 20, 1904, just over a year after it had begun, it was announced that the California Fruit Agency would be dissolved. The Southern California Fruit Exchange – now wiser and more experienced – would resume operations as a grower-owned organization on September 1. The Exchange was back in the hands of growers.

The Exchange recommenced its business with Woodford again in place as general manager. Story remained president. In a far-reaching move, the Exchange decided to expand beyond quality packing and the orderly distribution of fruit to market. Now the cooperative would expand its sales force and begin to actively convince retailers and wholesalers to handle only its fruit.

NORTHERN CITRUS GROWERS JOIN, CREATING THE
CALIFORNIA FRUIT GROWERS EXCHANGE

Meanwhile, citrus growers further north in the state's San Joaquin Valley were experiencing many of the same problems that had led their southern counterparts to form their own marketing organization some eleven years before. By 1905, these northern citrus growers had joined the ranks of the Exchange. To reflect its broadened membership, the Southern California Fruit Exchange changed its name. On March 27, 1905, it became the California Fruit Growers Exchange.

When it formally incorporated itself as the California Fruit Growers Exchange, the association re-adopted a firm tenet of basic cooperative principles. Its new by-laws stipulated that its board of directors must be comprised of persons "actively engaged in growing citrus fruit." Story was retained as president and Woodford as general manager.

By the end of the 1904-05 season, the Exchange could count 5,000 grower-members. It owned no citrus groves or property. It held no financial interest in packinghouses, district exchanges or other local property. All it owned was the furniture in its Los Angeles office. Yet, the association, with 45 percent of California's citrus industry, had watched its shipments total over 14,000 carloads, and returns hit a whopping $1.25 per box. Total returns topped $7 million – the highest it had ever seen. It was a season of success, and Chamblin's faith in grower-controlled citrus marketing had begun to pay off.

FRUIT GROWERS SUPPLY COMPANY

In 1907, the California Fruit Growers Exchange would add another branch to its grower-owned system. The devastating San Francisco earthquake and subsequent fire of 1906 had caused prices for timber to skyrocket as the city sought to re-build itself. Costs for wooden boxes for shipping citrus jumped. Frustrated by unsuccessful attempts to locate a steady supply of reasonably priced wood for packing crates, the California Fruit Growers Exchange again formed a self-help cooperative. This time, it created its own timber supply company – the Fruit Growers Supply Company.

When the Southern California Fruit Exchange had been formed in 1895, one of its stated purposes was to obtain "boxes, paper and other packing materials, fertilizers and other merchandise" for members. One of the items most needed was box shook for shipping crates, and it wasn't very easy to come by. As early as 1897, the district exchanges were asking the central organization for help. The problem was that most of the box shook manufacturers located anywhere near the citrus growing area were joined in a powerful cartel.

When demand for lumber leaped sky high in the wake of San Francisco's disaster, citrus growers learned the cost of their shipping boxes would jump by 75 percent. Balking at this, the growers joined forces with the Exchange to bypass cartel operations in Central

San Francisco earthquake – In the wake of San Francisco's devastating 1906 earthquake and fire, prices for timber skyrocketed. When manufacturers of wooden citrus crates raised their prices 75 percent, Exchange growers organized their own timber and crate-making business – the Fruit Growers Supply Co.

California. Instead, they began working with small, independent mills in Northern California.

In 1907, the district exchanges were given the authority to deduct three cents per box "to obtain packing supplies on the most advantageous terms." The buying operation they put together was Fruit Growers Supply Company. A lumber mill at Hilt in Northern California's Siskiyou County was obtained in 1910, and the new Exchange affiliate began to make boxes at great savings. The Supply Company would remain separate from the Exchange serving as a supply affiliate to the marketing association. Its first manager was a long-time Exchange employee, P.C. Daniels.

The Supply Company also made loans to mills, who, in return, would award lower-priced box contracts as well as interest to Exchange packinghouses. When one of these loans defaulted in 1910, the Supply Company took possession of 24,000 acres of timberland, a logging railroad, several sawmills, and a box factory. The property, near Hilt, California, helped the Supply Company maintain its control of box prices. In time, it would make available to members everything from wrappers and labels to orchard heaters, box shook and nails – all at reduced prices. By 1916, Supply Company orders reached more than $3 million per year.

ADVERTISING: "THE BEST INVESTMENT EVER MADE"

By 1907, the Exchange had begun to prosper. California orange shipments were headed for the 30,000 car mark – five times the volume of 1893. Partly because of increasingly heavy citrus production (which reportedly was even leading some growers to dig up their trees), the Exchange had begun advertising in earnest.

As MacCurdy records it in *The History Of The California Fruit Growers Exchange*, there had been reluctance among board members to expend money on advertising. Convinced that advertising should capitalize on California's appeal rather than just the name of the Exchange, directors feared outside shippers would benefit nearly as much as the cooperative's members under an Exchange-sponsored promotion.

"Some directors were certain that it was a great mistake," C.C. Teague remembered years later when he was president of the Exchange. "They were certain that if an advertising cost, of even a few cents a box, were deducted from the returns to growers, the Exchange would have difficulty in competing with other shippers who made no such deductions."

But others, like then-President Story, believed advertising, especially under the Exchange's brands, was essential. They felt consumption must be increased, or there would be a perpetual state of over-production and demoralization of markets. They also felt that since the Exchange was packing and selling its fruit at cost, it could still compete with independent shippers who added on a profit in their packing operations.

REDISCOVERY OF THE FIRST AD

"One of the interesting side lights of this 30th anniversary of Sunkist advertising was the re-discovery of the first Exchange advertisement. 'This first ad,' said (advertising manager) Mr. Geissinger, 'has been sort of a legend around here ever since anyone connected with the Exchange advertising can remember. There wasn't any copy of it in our office and Lord & Thomas, our agency who prepared it, didn't have a copy either. We didn't even know what size it was, just when it ran or where. But we decided inasmuch as 'Ding' illustrated it, it must have run in the *Des Moines Register*. We sent them a copy of the cartoon and asked them to make a hunt for it. Back in the musty files for March 2, 1908, they found it – a swell page ad. And what was our surprise to find that it ran in *three* colors – orange, green and black. The Register seemed to share our astonishment at that, too. Evidently this matter of color printing in newspapers isn't as new as we all thought.' "

For years, Story had been urging advertising action but without success. Then, sometime in 1907, Story talked the situation over with his friend, E.O. McCormick of the Southern Pacific Railway. The railroad was just as interested in moving people out West as the Exchange was in transporting oranges to the East. McCormick's "faith in the soundness of advertising was such that he told Story that for every dollar the Exchange expended in advertising, the railway he represented would spend an equal amount," MacCurdy wrote.

Although Exchange directors held some resentment against the railroad for what they felt were exorbitant freight rates and thought the proposed amount "dreadfully extravagant," they authorized management in 1907 an amount not to exceed $10,000 in the advertising of citrus fruits.

Following this authorization, the Exchange's first major advertising campaign was launched. It marked the first time a perishable food product was ever advertised. Working with an advertising agency known as Lord & Thomas (now Foote, Cone and Belding), the Exchange developed a three-color newspaper ad – in black, green and orange – promoting its oranges. The ad, containing a cartoon by J.N. "Ding" Darling, would be placed in the *Des Moines Register*. In fact, the Iowa city was selected as the center point of the campaign.

The first week of March, 1908 was declared "Orange Week in Iowa." The ad announced that the area would be receiving "direct from the beautiful groves of California hundreds of carloads of the choicest oranges grown in the world." Fruit was shipped to Iowa in special bannered trains, and prizes were offered for articles that could be used in advertising California oranges and lemons. Southern Pacific posted billboards throughout Iowa to display such slogans as, "Oranges for health – California for wealth." A prominent lecturer was employed to tour Iowa's larger cities to elaborate on California's many advantages, especially its orange industry.

The campaign cost less than $7,000 but proved its worth many times over. Sales before the Iowa campaign were carefully checked. While business for the country as a whole increased almost 20 percent, business in Iowa alone gained a stunning 50 percent. By September 1908, Exchange directors were so convinced by the results, they increased funding to $25,000 to be used for advertising that season. Six million stickers reading "Sunkist Oranges" and one million reading "Sunkist Lemons" were ordered in the fall of 1908 to be pasted on the regular labels of Exchange shippers.

BRANDING NATURE'S PRODUCT

It was during the preparations for the Iowa campaign that the trademark "Sunkist" was first suggested for advertisement rather than using just the Exchange name. Exchange officials, realizing they needed a high-quality appeal to the public, sought a catchy description of the fruit for Exchange box labels. Some members opposed this, asserting that

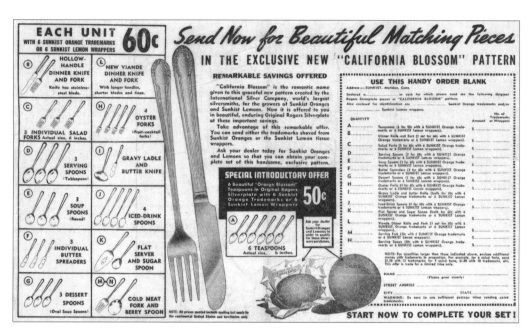

In 1908, the California Fruit Growers Exchange introduced a promotional gift to consumers, offering its specially-designed "Orange Blossom" silverware in exchange for the Sunkist-marked tissues that wrapped fruit. The promotion was so successful that the cooperative would become the single largest purchaser of flat silverware in the world.

dealers had already become accustomed to a number of well-known individual labels. But it was obvious the Exchange had a need for uniformity in its advertising.

MacCurdy wrote that it was an R.C. Brandon of the Lord & Thomas agency who, back in July 1907, had first suggested using "Sunkissed." A month later, the spelling "Sunkist" was being advocated. And although it was too late in the planning stages to use the new name in the Iowa campaign, the "Sunkist" name had captured the organization's interest. In April 1908, the board agreed to adopt the word "Sunkist" as its trademark to appear on the boxes of the association's best grades of fruit.

To ensure that the Sunkist trademark would be exclusively associated with the Exchange, a plan also was developed to stamp the paper wrapper that enveloped each piece of fruit with the "Sunkist" name. And to make sure that those wrappers stayed on the fruit until the consumer bought it, the Exchange offered a promotional gift. For every twelve wrappers and twelve cents a consumer turned in, he or she would receive a sharp-pointed spoon for eating oranges cut in half. Thousands of orders poured in, causing the Exchange to add knives and forks to the offer.

"Many a bride in the period 1910 to 1917 started her silver service with the Orange Blossom silverware offered by the Exchange," *The Sunkist Courier* recalled many years later. "So popular was the offer that the orders for spoons reached the staggering total of over 5,000 per day. The Exchange became the largest single purchaser of flat silverware in the world."

THE EXCHANGE EXPANDS

By 1910, the organization's membership comprised over 60 percent of California's citrus industry. It counted some 6,500 orange and lemon growers in its membership. Its returns approached $15 million a year. Some 20,000 carloads of citrus fruit were shipped to market. That season, navel oranges – the Exchange's biggest volume crop – earned over $1.50 per box while valencias brought in nearly $2.25. And with the acquisition by the Fruit Growers Supply Company of the lumber mill near Hilt, Exchange members could easily meet their requirements of some six million wooden boxes a year.

The mood all over California was upbeat. The state's population had skyrocketed to 2.4 million people, almost a million more than 10 years before. Los Angeles held almost 320,000 people. Helped by good weather and improving transportation methods – including the growing appeal of the automobile – California's citrus farmers prospered. So did their marketing cooperative.

With its ever-increasing reputation based on the uniform quality of its oranges and lemons, the Exchange began to expand its operations. Its year-round fresh-fruit marketing – navels in the winter, valencias in the summer, lemons all year – helped its Los Angeles office, located in the Consolidated Realty Building, become a nerve center of market infor-

Each packinghouse belonged to a district exchange. The exchanges were in daily contact with Exchange headquarters in the Consolidated Realty Building in downtown Los Angeles.

Left: By 1910, the Exchange had begun sending inspectors to packinghouses to ensure that fruit packed under the Sunkist name was of the highest quality.   Right: By 1912, the Exchange was shipping over 9 million boxes of fruit a season.

mation, sales orders, and shipping instructions. There was constant communication between the Exchange and its packinghouse members as well as its Eastern sales representatives.

The Exchange began sending its employees to supervise handling operations at the packinghouses. Sometimes, according to Exchange board minutes of January 1910, a special inspector was employed "to visit all of our packinghouses when in operation and make investigation and observations of what quality and grade of fruit is being packed under the different brands, particularly as to what is being packed under the brands bearing the Sunkist trademark." In 1910, the Exchange developed a claims department which evolved into a traffic department. It opened a sales office in London, England and began regular export shipments.

The various packinghouses (or associations) maintained their own district exchange which represented them in their dealings with the central office in Los Angeles.

In 1910, the cooperative employed some 200 people; that number would expand to 250 two years later. The general manager received the highest salary at $1,000 per month; department heads earned from $350 to $500.

During the 1911-12 season, the Exchange shipped 9,191,143 boxes, netting almost $17 million for its 6,000 members, or an average of $1.84 per box (F.O.B. Calif.) It depended largely on its General Eastern office in Chicago for sales and to coordinate its advertising. The Exchange maintained its office in Buffalo, New York, which had sold 3,022 cars of citrus fruit during the 1910-11 season.

Yet the cooperative kept its costs down. By 1912, even with increased advertising, Exchange expenses were held to a mere seven cents per box, according to a report from the cooperative's general manager, B.A. Woodford. In his last report to Exchange directors and members in August 1912, the ailing Woodford said, "During the last three years, your advertising campaign has added about one cent to your expenses which, in my opinion, is the best investment you have ever made."

POWELL IS GREETED BY THE 1913 FREEZE

In 1912, B.A. Woodford stepped down after eight years as general manager of the Exchange and an even longer history with the Lemon Growers Exchange. His replacement was G. Harold Powell, a former official of the U.S. Department of Agriculture.

It was Powell who had headed an investigation back in 1904 into the reasons for the costly decay that had been taking between $500,000 and $1,500,000 a year from California citrus growers. Undertaken at the request of the industry, the investigation was spearheaded by Powell's employer, the U.S. Department of Agriculture. Powell's four-year investigation would prove that the decay was caused by blue-mold fungus entering oranges through mechanical injuries to the skin from clipper cuts, stem punctures, scratches and

Lasting several nights, the 1913 freeze forced growers to burn their orchard heaters all night to try to save their trees. Workers then spent all day refilling the heaters. Local oil refineries worked overtime to turn out oil for the heaters. "Everyone was ready to drop from fatigue," grower C.C. Teague would later write.

The freeze that hit Southern California between December 1912 and January 1913 is considered one of the worst the area has ever known. The region's citrus crop dropped from an expected 10 million boxes to just 4 million.

By 1915, the Exchange's advertising budget totaled $250,000 per year. Recipes and suggestions for additional citrus uses were prominent in Exchange advertising, headquartered at that time in Chicago.

bruises. The discovery led to a radical change in handling operations throughout the industry, and a virtual end to the decay problem.

Powell took over as general manager of the California Fruit Growers Exchange just in time to see Southern California's citrus industry experience the worst freeze it had ever known. Between December 1912 and January 1913, temperatures as low as 20 degrees Fahrenheit brought severe damage to as much as 39 percent of the citrus crop in the state's southern regions.

"I often think of the fight and the inadequate facilities we had in the freeze of 1913," C.C. Teague of the Limoneira Ranch near Santa Paula wrote many years later. "The freeze lasted several nights. The oil in the heaters would burn completely out during the night and they had to be refilled the next day. This required much labor and the men were forced to work day and night with almost no sleep. Everyone connected with the operation was ready to drop with fatigue and loss of sleep and only the loyalty of our men saved our crop."

To head off further damage, Powell managed to convince local oil refineries to work overtime to turn out fuel for orchard heaters. And although these arrangements prevented further losses to the citrus crop, the damage had been done. The region's expected 10-million-box crop dropped to 4 million.

Outside shippers rushed to sell the fruit. News of the freeze-marred fruit reached Eastern markets, and sales of California citrus withered while Florida took the lead. But rather than ship damaged fruit and lose its high-quality reputation with Eastern wholesalers and retailers, the Exchange forbade its packinghouses to make shipments. The Exchange cut its operating costs by 50 percent, reducing salaries, lowering advertising budgets and laying off dispensable employees.

Although doomsayers predicted that the freeze signaled the end of Southern California's citrus industry, its growers bounced back to produce a bumper crop in the 1913-14 season. That year, with the help of its exclusive agents in principal U.S. markets, its advertising, and the unsurpassed flavor of its oranges, the Exchange re-gained its status in the marketplace.

Despite the low citrus prices that prevailed on the uncertain eve of World War I, Exchange business continued to grow in the East. The cooperative had expanded its divisions, now operating a Northeastern, an Atlantic, a Central and a Northern Division. In 1914, a Southern and a Northwestern Division were also added.

In 1914, the Exchange established a dealer service department to build its citrus sales. The early dealer service men made personal visits to retailers, demonstrating proper display of fruit and showing how to figure costs and selling price to obtain the greatest volume.

WORLD WAR I

The outbreak of war in Europe in 1914 inflated the American economy, bringing high inflation and both strong demand and prices for citrus. With some of the prosperity reaching citrus farmers, the Exchange directors decided they could afford to budget in additional funds for advertising. Maybe it was time to overcome the perception that oranges and lemons were luxury items. Little did they realize the forces their advertising would stir.

By 1915, the Exchange's total advertising budget had increased to $250,000 a year, and it was branching into color ads in famous national magazines, such as the *Saturday Evening Post* and *Ladies Home Journal.* Under Exchange advertising expert Don Francisco, the ads highlighted California's beautiful terrain and lovely young women picking oranges. The ads also carried coupons for cook books, recipes or suggestions for uses of citrus.

But citrus growers had begun to realize that marketing all citrus as fresh fruit was not going to be economical. The Exchange membership was producing some 12 million boxes of oranges and lemons a year. "Our fruit is produced by 8,000 growers," Powell reported. "It must be consumed by 100 million people."

The Exchange began to seek other ways to market its growing citrus crop. In 1915, its new dealer service was sending representatives to work closely with buyers. That year, too, the cooperative bought a small marmalade factory in Ontario, fifty miles east of Los Angeles. The plant was remodeled and machinery installed for producing citric acid and flavorings made from orange and lemon oils. Within two years, the Ontario plant was producing over 175,000 pounds of citric acid and 1,000 gallons of oil each year.

EXCHANGE EXPANDS INTO LEMON BY-PRODUCTS

That same year, 1915, the Exchange lemon shippers organized a company to manufacture by-products from lower grades of fruit. Known as the Exchange By-Products Company, it constructed a plant in Corona, Calif., to process lemons for citric acid and lemon oil. Although its membership was the same as the California Fruit Growers Exchange, the new organization would maintain a separate board of directors. "The business will be handled on a co-operative basis," Powell reported, "the growers receiving the full returns for the by-products after the cost of operation is deducted." Later, citrus pectin was added and eventually a complete line of juice and peel products was developed.

By seeking ways to develop citrus by-products, the Exchange had found a market outlet for poorer qualities of its fruit. Using everything from peel to pulp, by-products processing not only expanded markets but helped limit the potential of lower prices that could result with too much fresh fruit going to market. And the Exchange had achieved this without interfering with production. Soon, it found another avenue for citrus consumption.

The forerunner of the Sunkist lemon products division in Corona, California as it looked in 1929.

Upper left: The Exchange's marmalade factory near Ontario, purchased in 1915, soon began to manufacture citrus by-products, such as citric acid and flavorings.   Upper right: The forerunner of Sunkist's Products division, the early by-products operations marked the first time citrus by-products were made into consumer products.   Lower left: Women cut and peel fruit for processing into one of many by-products, such as citric acid.   Lower right: Jars are filled with marmalade to be marketed.

THE EXCHANGE INTRODUCES ORANGE JUICE

Up until this point, orange juice was virtually unknown. Oranges were eaten on the half-shell, or sliced or eaten out of hand. The Exchange would forever change that.

In 1916, one of the most famous campaigns the Exchange was ever to promote began appearing in its national advertising efforts. The "Drink An Orange" campaign marked the first time orange juice was promoted. Because there were no juice extractors large enough for oranges on the market, the Exchange assisted in the development and distribution of the devices. It persuaded a glass company to produce a million glass reamers for the Exchange to distribute through retail outlets. Glass hand-juicers were offered for 10 cents each. Not only did the squeezers sell out within the year, but all manufacturers of glass extractors were soon making ones similar to the Exchange's.

The "Drink An Orange" campaign directed by the Exchange's Don Francisco, exceeded all expectations. It saw consumption of oranges increase from half an orange per serving to 2-3 per serving. At the same time, the Exchange's lemon advertising promoted the fruit's uses for lemonade, cooking, mouth wash, cosmetic purposes, laundry, and household cleaning. This spurred increased production in both Florida and California. And it helped change the perception of oranges and lemons as luxury items into recognition of the fruit as a diet staple.

Juice advertising became one of the most powerful innovations the Exchange ever introduced. And, in addition to non-Exchange members, others benefited by the idea. Producers of tomatoes, grapes, apples and prunes soon followed what the Exchange had done.

In 1917, California's citrus industry was bringing in almost $48 million dollars to the state. California had set a new record by supplying 71 percent of the lemons consumed in America. Few could deny that the Exchange – representing 69 percent of the state's citrus volume – was responsible for the healthy business. The Exchange even helped achieve the passing of a law by the California legislature to provide a maturity standard on oranges that would regulate quality. In 1917, the Exchange also adopted standards that would allow grapefruit to be included in the "Sunkist" grade.

That year, too, the Exchange established a monthly publication, *The Sunkist Courier*. Edited by Don Francisco, *The Sunkist Courier* would keep the 8,000 Exchange grower-members informed of important happenings in their industry, markets, and organization. In January 1918, *The Sunkist Courier* would merge with *The California Citrograph*, a newsletter which reported on the cultural side of the citrus industry.

During this time, the sales force of the Exchange numbered 150 men in 59 offices throughout the country, all working to enlarge the cooperative's markets. "This sales force is in touch with 2,500 fruit jobbers who, through something like 7,500 salesmen, sell to 300,000 retailers in every nook and corner of the country," *The Sunkist Courier* reported. Yet, the Exchange held its total average operating cost in 1917 to a mere 4.75 cents per box – the lowest in its history.

A remembrance of history surfaced in 1917 when P.J. Dreher – founder of the Claremont Association and one of the Exchange creators – retired as secretary and manager of the San Antonio Fruit Exchange after 22 years of service. Later that year, Nathan Blanchard of Santa Paula died. Regarded as one of the pioneers and strong leaders of Ventura County's citrus industry, Blanchard had founded the Limoneira Ranch, which became the world's largest lemon producer. He was 86.

THE DEMANDS OF WAR

World War I directly affected the citrus industry in connection with its labor supply, wages, materials, and freight rates. The demands of war absorbed very large amounts of citrus as well as lumber for boxes to ship the fruit in. Often there were shortages of materials, rail cars and labor. The Exchange also felt the War's impact as 36 of its employees joined the country's fighting forces. Although many of them fought at the Front, none would be killed. And in July 1917, the Exchange was requested by U.S. President Herbert Hoover to contribute the services of general manager Powell to organize the Perishable Food Division of the government's Food Administration. E.G. Dezell would act as Exchange Manager until Powell returned in 1919.

By the time the Armistice was signed in Europe on November 11, 1918, the Exchange had become widely known as an innovator in the advertising field. Each year, the growers' organization was distributing over 500 million advertisements through over 20 magazines and 400 daily newspapers.

In fact, the Exchange was expanding in every way. By 1919, its annual revenue approached $57 million. Its 10,000 members produced almost 75 percent of the citrus in California. Its affiliated cooperative, the Fruit Growers Supply Company, would acquire over 41,000 acres of virgin forest in Lassen County that year to assure its growers a future supply of shipping boxes at reasonable prices. The Exchange's distribution of fruit represented the most highly developed system of organized marketing in American agriculture. The Sunkist trademark, whether it accompanied valencias, navels or lemons, was synonymous with quality.

As the decade closed, there was no longer a "season" for California citrus. Summer-ripening valencias, winter-harvested navels and year-round lemons made fresh-fruit shipments possible throughout the year. For growers, there would always be Mother Nature's ongoing freezes, heat waves or strong winds to damage or scar their fruit. But now growers had a defense of their own. The marketing organization they had built in desperation over 25 years earlier had become a giant and its brand name a household word.

Fruit Growers Supply Company added to its timberland holdings by purchasing 41,000 acres of virgin forest in Lassen County in 1919.

The Exchange became widely known as an innovator in advertising, distributing over 500 million advertisements through over 20 magazines and 400 daily newspapers. Recipes and suggestions for ways to use citrus were often featured.

CHAPTER IV – The 1920s

GREAT STRIDES

C.C. Teague, president of the Exchange board from 1920-1950. Teague, a grower from Santa Paula, California, headed up farming operations for the Limoneira Ranch before becoming Limoneira's president in 1917.

One of the first events of the Twenties was the ending of F.Q. Story's 23-year career as president of the Exchange. Story had seen the cooperative through its days when sales brought in only $12 million during the 1906-07 season. By 1920, with its great strides in advertising, the organization was earning nearly $60 million in a season.

In recognition of Story's contributions to the association and the industry, the board of directors named him Honorary Life President. Upon his retirement in March 1920 at the age of 75, Story was honored with these words, "In his relations with the board, he has presided and led with a fine courtesy and an appreciation of the rights of members that has endeared him to them; in his relations with the district exchanges and the associations, he has acted with a singular, detached disinterestedness, but with fairness to each; and in his kindly, sympathetic relations and interest in the employees of the organization, he has been a source of cherished inspiration."

For the next six months, P.J. Dreher – the man behind the Claremont organization which had contributed so much to the cooperative citrus movement in California – would serve as president. Then, in September 1920, Charles Collins Teague of Santa Paula was named to the Exchange's top post. Teague would remain president for 30 years, until his death in 1950.

Fate had brought Teague to the citrus industry in August 1893 – the same month and year the Exchange had been formed. Teague's father had died that month, leaving the 20-year-old young man to support his mother and two sisters. Immediately, Teague found work with Nathan Blanchard, the pioneer lemon grower in Ventura County. Over time, the young man learned every facet of citrus production, and eventually went into the lemon-growing business himself. He helped develop the famous Limoneira Ranch, which would become the world's largest lemon producer.

Under Teague's leadership, the Exchange moved into ever-greater advertising. In 1920, its advertising budget reached $500,000 a year. That year, the cooperative became the first national advertiser to mention vitamins in its ad copy, with special emphasis on Vitamin C. The word "vitamine" was just being introduced to the public as medical research was discovering this new group of dietary essentials. Researchers reported that "vitamines" were essential to the maintenance of good health, and one in particular, the one called Vitamin C, could be found in abundant amounts in citrus fruit.

Focusing on the healthful properties of citrus, the Exchange leaped on the new-found attribute of its products. Its advertising spread the word of the health benefits of Vitamin C and citrus fruit. To verify the soundness of its claims, the Exchange urged consumers to show its ads to doctors so that their medical endorsements would add to parents' confidence in citrus for their children's health.

This kind of advertising was not only building markets, but enhancing the reputation of the Exchange with growers. By 1920, Exchange membership totaled 12,000 growers from some 230 local associations, or 75 percent of the state's citrus volume. More than 190,000 acres of California land were planted to orange and lemon trees, and 50,000 carloads of fruit were being marketed annually. The orange crop, noted Albert J. Meyer in his *History of the California Fruit Growers Exchange, 1893-1920,* brought in $60 million a year, making it California's second-largest income earner after oil.

Keeping pace with the growing industry, packinghouses had become modernized. By 1920, most of them were hooked up to power that carried fruit along conveyer belts for sizing, washing, waxing, and grading. From there, the fruit moved into accumulation bins for tissue wrap and packing in the 75-pound wooden boxes. It took more than 200 packinghouses in the Exchange system to do the job.

The growth of the industry – and the resulting need for expanded supplies – led the Fruit Growers Supply Company to build another lumber mill in 1921, this one in Susanville, California. Shipments now amounted to 15 million wooden boxes annually.

EXCHANGE ESTABLISHES ORANGE BY-PRODUCTS DIVISION

And as far as the Exchange was concerned, there was more room for growth. Taking its cue from the Exchange Lemon Products Company, the Exchange established in 1921 a by-products organization to utilize oranges not suitable for fresh-fruit shipments. Located first in San Dimas, California, and later in nearby Ontario, this organization became the Exchange Orange Products Company. It worked to develop by-products such as concentrated orange juice, peel products, and pulp for dairy feed. In 1922, the Exchange scored another first in California citrus history when it made the first export shipments of orange oil, these going to Canada and England.

The Exchange had already, in 1921, successfully shipped oranges to the Atlantic seaboard via the Panama Canal. It had been considering the idea of "water shipment" even before World War I, and now, as ships were released from war uses, the Exchange began experimenting with major overseas shipments of oranges and lemons. In April, the Exchange launched the first direct by-water shipment of California oranges and lemons from Los Angeles to London. The shipment, valued at $21,000, included selected boxes of Sunkist oranges and lemons for the King and Queen of England.

Neither of these ventures pleased the railroads. As business through the Panama Canal increased, railroads proposed a 10 percent reduction on freight rates to citrus growers if they would boycott the canal route. Powell refused the railroads' proposal.

As water shipments took off, the Exchange increased its exports. It began shipping fruit to the Orient and Honolulu via San Francisco. The volume of fruit increased steadily to China, the Philippines, Japan, and even Australia and New Zealand.

A 1926 view of The Exchange Orange Products Company in Ontario, where culled oranges were made into concentrated orange juice, peel products, and pulp for dairy feed.

In April 1921, the Exchange launched the first direct by-water shipment of oranges and lemons from Los Angeles to London via the Panama Canal.   Inset: Crates of citrus are loaded into the ship's hold. Valued at $21,000, this first direct water shipment to London included selected boxes of Sunkist oranges and lemons for the King and Queen of England.

INTERNAL CHANGES

Meanwhile, changes were underway within the Exchange. In April 1921, the board of directors of the Exchange appointed Paul S. Armstrong to the position of advertising manager. Armstrong had joined the Exchange in 1916 as a member of the dealer service department in Boston.

Later that year, the Exchange moved its offices to the seventh and eighth floors of the Consolidated Realty Building in downtown Los Angeles.

By March 1922, Sunkist management was under general manager Earl G. Dezell, who had assumed his post after the sudden death of Powell a month before. Powell had been a giant in agricultural circles throughout the U.S. Upon Powell's death, even U.S. President Warren G. Harding "expressed . . . great admiration for Mr. Powell's personality and ability, and explained to Mrs. Harding the great work Powell had done in forwarding the cooperative movement," according to a Feb. 22, 1922 letter from A.D. Lasker, chairman of the U.S. Shipping Board.

New manager Dezell had been with the Exchange almost since its inception, beginning work "as an office boy in knee pants," *The Sunkist Courier* reported. As former assistant to both Woodford and Powell, Dezell understood how important increased citrus consumption was to the Exchange.

Dezell continued the cooperative's philosophy of working closely with the retail trade to encourage grocers not just to sell oranges, but to display them where consumers could easily see them.

"Good display, reasonable margin and rapid turnover are axioms in the merchandising of fruit," Dezell reported in 1923, which was why the Exchange employed its dealer service force. These men called on thousands of retail stores, disseminating practical sales advice based on careful observation and study of effective fruit-selling methods throughout the country. The dealer service men distributed Sunkist display material that highlighted the Exchange's "Sunkist" and "Red Ball" trademarked brands. They also personally arranged displays in most of the stores they visited.

The 1920s saw the Exchange promoting orange juice consumption by focusing on nutrition and the value of orange juice to young, growing children. The Exchange advertising strategy responded to mothers' concerns for protecting their children against colds and pneumonia by emphasizing the nutritional value of citrus. Orange juice was publicized for adults as well.

In 1922, there were an estimated 60,000 soda fountains in the country – practically an untouched marked for oranges and lemons. That year, the Exchange manufactured and sold thousands of Sunkist Electric Fruit Juice Extractors to soda fountain establishments across the U.S., thus introducing on a large scale fresh fruit orangeade and lemonade to

A typical 1938 Sunkist fruit display in Houston, Texas emphasized "record crop sales."

Left: In the early 1920s, motion picture stars like Claire Windsor were used to help promote orangeade and lemonade made with Sunkist Juice Extractors.   Right: "America's Sweetheart," silent film star Mary Pickford, poses at a soda fountain in this early 1920s photo. She is drinking a glass of fresh orange juice made with a Sunkist Juice Extractor.

these retail outlets. The market grew to include hotels, cafes, hospitals and ice-cream manufacturers.

ORDERLY DISTRIBUTION AND CAPPER-VOLSTEAD

Even then, in 1922, before marketing orders were put into law, the Exchange was supporting the method of orderly distribution of fruit. "A regular, dependable supply tends to stabilize market conditions and to place the business of the trade on a less hazardous basis, enabling them to operate on smaller margins and to devote their time and energies chiefly to distribution," Dezell wrote in his 1922 annual report. "It gives the consumer the fruit in its best possible condition and at lowest average prices. Nobody benefits by gluts, famines and fluctuations in markets resulting from improper distribution."

In 1922, a piece of legislation critical to agriculture and the Exchange was passed by Congress. The Capper-Volstead Act gave agricultural marketing cooperatives a firm legal foundation, a limited exemption from the nation's anti-trust laws. The Exchange pronounced its support of this law. "This statute ... reflects the feeling of producers throughout the country that they should have the right to organize in order to act collectively in the doing of those things which they would otherwise be required to do as individuals, but which in many cases they could not accomplish alone."

BY-PRODUCTS HELP EXCHANGE THRIVE

By 1924, the Lemon Products Company's factory at Corona was producing thousands of pounds of lemon oil, crystallized citric acid, and its newest star, pectin. Developed by the Exchange's Research Laboratory, finished pectin in its dry powder form was the purest, most concentrated product of its kind ever offered the jelly-making trade. And The Exchange Orange Products Company in Ontario was thriving too, with customers not only in the U.S. but in Europe and Australia too. Sales of raw and concentrated juices, orange oils, pectin, and especially soda-water bottlers' products showed favorable increases. California orange juice had become the national summer drink.

The 1924-25 season produced the greatest returns to California for the citrus fruit crop in its history. The state's citrus crop returned almost $94 million – $70 million of it through the Exchange.

It happened again the next two seasons. The 1925-26 season not only broke all records for volume of California's citrus shipments – over 25 million boxes of oranges, lemons, and grapefruit were shipped – but the crop returned a whopping $98 million to the Golden State. The Exchange announced that its Sunkist Electric Fruit Juice Extractor was responsible for the consumption of nearly 1.7 million boxes, which were converted into orange juice and lemonade. By-products were becoming such a large part of

Exchange business that in 1926, the lemon and orange products companies combined sales under one management, marketing through the Exchange name.

During the 1926-27 season, shipments by California citrus growers returned a record $120 million to the state. The estimated retail value of the crop was $255 million. "Each American family spent an average of $9.33 for California citrus fruits," the Exchange reported.

By the middle of the decade, the California Fruit Growers Exchange had 22 directors on its board. This board met every Wednesday. In addition to general manager Dezell, the cooperative also had a general counsel, an orange and a lemon sales agent, a traffic manager, a field manager, an advertising manager and an auditor, all heading up their own departments. One dynamic staff member was Dana C. King, who had been orange sales manager since 1913. In 1922, the Exchange had added a Growers' Services Bureau to its Field Department to familiarize citrus growers with the work of the cooperative.

In the late 1920s, the Exchange sponsored the first-ever commercial radio broadcast between California and the East Coast. In doing so, the organization became the first to use motion picture stars in radio programs. One series of broadcasts in 1929 ran every Wednesday evening for half an hour. The program featured "colorful Spanish music, interspersed with announcements on the superior richness, healthfulness and flavor of Sunkist oranges and orange juice," according to Dezell's annual report.

The cooperative was connected with 23 district exchanges and 204 associations which made up the Exchange organization. They were located as far south as San Diego to as far north as Oroville. By 1929, Arizona citrus growers also were marketing through the Exchange. Desert grapefruit growers in the Imperial and Yuma valleys formed a district organization, "Desert Citrus Exchange," in 1929 to make a specialty of marketing the superior grapefruit of the desert. By September 1929, the "Desert District Exchange" was welcomed as a new district exchange member of the California Fruit Growers Exchange.

The Exchange's six divisions were headquartered from coast to coast, and its district managers covered nearly every major city in America, and even a few in Canada. By 1926, the Exchange had 84 district sales offices, and a total of 390 employees. By telegram, telephone, letter and personal contact, the Exchange kept the flow of information coming in and out of its Los Angeles headquarters. In fact, the Exchange had its own telegraph department. During the 1925-26 season, the Exchange received over 32,000 wires, and sent out over 37,000 – practically all of them in the cooperative's private code.

"The Exchange organization has the responsibility for the proper movement and distribution of the crop, the development of markets, the improvement of trade practices and merchandising methods and for increasing consumption," general manager Dezell explained, "and is the controlling factor in improving standards of quality and uniformity of pack."

SUNKIST NAME APPEARS ON FRUIT AND IN THE GROVES

In a revolutionary step, the Exchange announced in November 1926 that the new season would commence with the name "Sunkist" being stamped directly on its oranges, bypassing the paper tissues that had traditionally wrapped the fruit. Under the new system, oranges would pass through one of the electrical marking machines, which would be placed at the end of the grader. Fruit of all sizes would receive the "indelible" Sunkist brand and go on to the sizers and packing bins. The eight-run machine could mark two carloads of some 200,000 individual oranges as a normal day's work, at a cost of less than one cent per box.

The Sunkist name was also promoted out in growers' groves. "Sunkist growers, new and old, are proud to identify their groves by using the standard Sunkist grove signs," *The Sunkist Courier* proclaimed. The signs, enameled on iron in three colors, were 18 inches long, and were made to order. Some of the signs just said, "Sunkist Grove." Others included not only the grower's name and ranch but also his or her packinghouse. The more complete signs could be purchased through the Exchange for $1.45 each.

In a revolutionary move, oranges were stamped with the Sunkist name for the first time in November 1926, eliminating the tissue wrapper which once carried the brand name. "This machine will mark 2 carloads of approximately 200,000 individual oranges as a normal day's work, with no additional labor and at a total cost of less than one cent per box." the Exchange reported.

Members continued to benefit from the Fruit Growers Supply Company. By 1927 – its 20th anniversary – the Supply Company was purchasing $10 million worth of orchard and packing supplies for its members a year. Its aggregate sum of purchases over its 20 years was $104 million. Operated at cost, the Supply Company now had a purchasing division in Los Angeles and a lumber division with offices in San Francisco for the operation of the lumber plants and sale of their products. Its timber holdings and mills were located in Siskiyou and Lassen Counties in Northern California.

By 1927, Exchange exports to Europe had skyrocketed. That year, shipments reached 500,000 boxes – nearly as great as the previous 16 years combined. At times, 10 percent of Exchange shipments were exported. All European business was handled through an Exchange sales office in London.

In April 1929, the Mediterranean fruit fly was discovered in Florida, presenting a new and serious menace. California authorities immediately strengthened the inspection service by rail and road to intercept the entry of Florida fruits, and made an intensive survey to make sure the fly had not already entered the state. California also cooperated in requesting the federal government to supply funds for the eradication of the pest in Florida. The eradication campaign was successful but quarantines remained in effect against the shipment of Florida fruit into southern and western states.

In July 1929, Exchange President Teague had been appointed a member of the Federal Farm Board, created out of the Agricultural Marketing Act to assist farmers in depressed industries. He would spend considerable time in Washington, D.C. in this position, as did George Farrand, Exchange general counsel. This would build valuable contacts and rapport for the Exchange.

As the decade closed, the Exchange had 11,000 members and nearly 78 percent of California's citrus crop. Its services, excluding advertising, cost members an average of 6.68 cents per box. The cost of the national advertising campaign was met by an assessment of 5 cents per box on oranges and 10 cents on lemons and grapefruit.

Despite the stock market crash of 1929, the Exchange capped the Roaring Twenties with this boast. "In the face of adverse business conditions and depressed buying power throughout the United States during the marketing season of 1929-30," the Exchange reported, "the results of this year clearly indicate the cumulative value of 23 years of national advertising and merchandising effort behind the Exchange fruit."

The Exchange's pioneering days were definitely over.

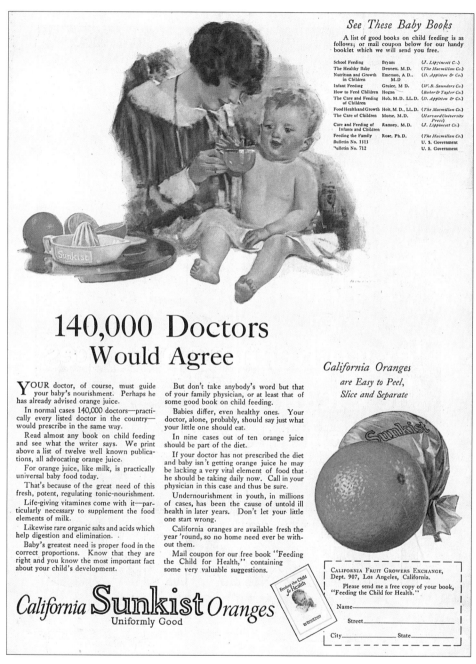

140,000 Doctors
Would Agree

YOUR doctor, of course, must guide your baby's nourishment. Perhaps he has already advised orange juice.

In normal cases 140,000 doctors—practically every listed doctor in the country—would prescribe in the same way.

Read almost any book on child feeding and see what the writer says. We print above a list of twelve well known publications, all advocating orange juice.

For orange juice, like milk, is practically universal baby food today.

That's because of the great need of this fresh, potent, regulating tonic-nourishment.

Life-giving vitamines come with it—particularly necessary to supplement the food elements of milk.

Likewise rare organic salts and acids which help digestion and elimination. .

Baby's greatest need is proper food in the correct proportions. Know that they are right and you know the most important fact about your child's development.

But don't take anybody's word but that of your family physician, or at least that of some good book on child feeding.

Babies differ, even healthy ones. Your doctor, alone, probably, should say just what your little one should eat.

In nine cases out of ten orange juice should be part of the diet.

If your doctor has not prescribed the diet and baby isn't getting orange juice he may be lacking a very vital element of food that he should be taking daily now. Call in your physician in this case and thus be sure.

Undernourishment in youth, in millions of cases, has been the cause of untold ill health in later years. Don't let your little one start wrong.

California oranges are available fresh the year 'round, so no home need ever be without them.

Mail coupon for our free book "Feeding the Child for Health," containing some very valuable suggestions.

California Oranges are Easy to Peel, Slice and Separate

California **Sunkist** *Oranges*
Uniformly Good

In the 1920s, the Exchange's advertising strategy responded to mothers' concerns for protecting their children against illness by focusing on the nutritional value of orange juice.

"SUPPOSE YOU HAD TO GO IT ALONE"
A MESSAGE
TO CITRUS GROWERS

Suppose there was no California Fruit Growers Exchange
and you had to "go it alone" in packing, shipping,
selling and advertising your fruit.

Could you build your own packing plant?

Would you have sufficient volume to operate a
packinghouse efficiently?

Could you maintain your own private salesmen
in all the important markets of the country?

Could you educate one hundred and twenty million people
to eat more oranges and lemons to insure your market?

Could you control and popularize a brand like "Sunkist"
so that people everywhere would specify and get your fruit?

Could you develop by-products and build markets for them
that would return a profit on unmarketable fruit?

These are but a few of the services that the
California Fruit Growers Exchange renders you today.

And the total cost is only a few cents a box.

No longer does the speculator buy oranges and lemons for less
than the cost of producing them.
No longer is the industry in doubt.

60,000 cars of citrus fruit are shipped out of California in a year
because the Exchange has made that possible.

A million dollars or more in cash is returned to
California citrus growers every week through the
energy of the Exchange and the miracle of co-operation.

Most growers prosper because they know the folly of
trying to "go it alone"
and the strength of working together.

The Sunkist Courier, February 1926

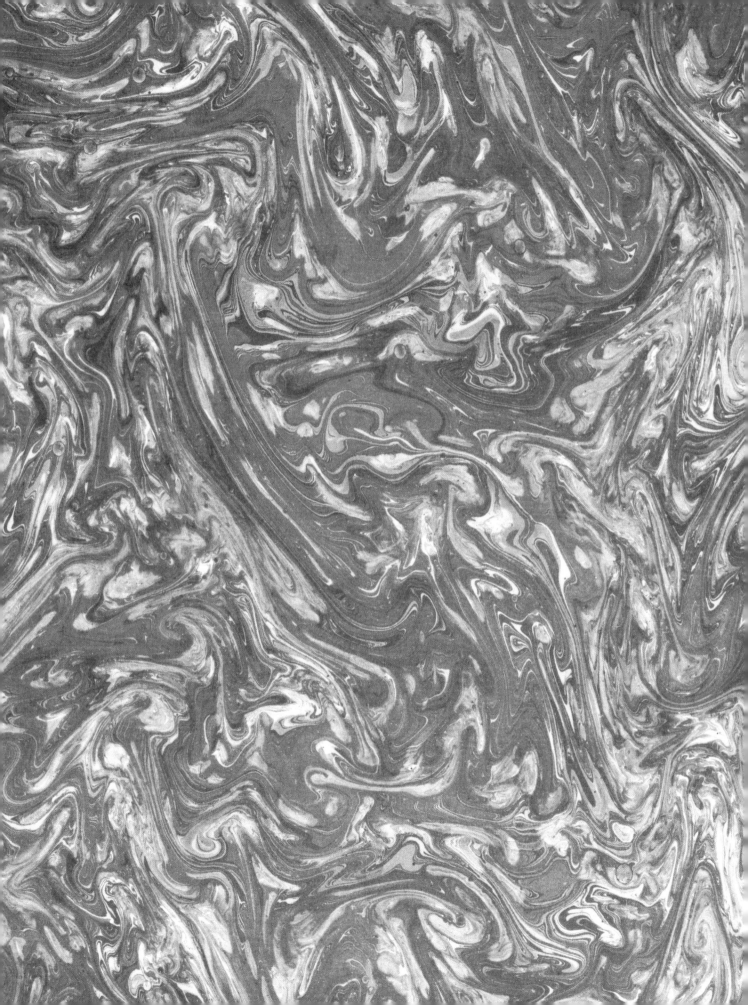

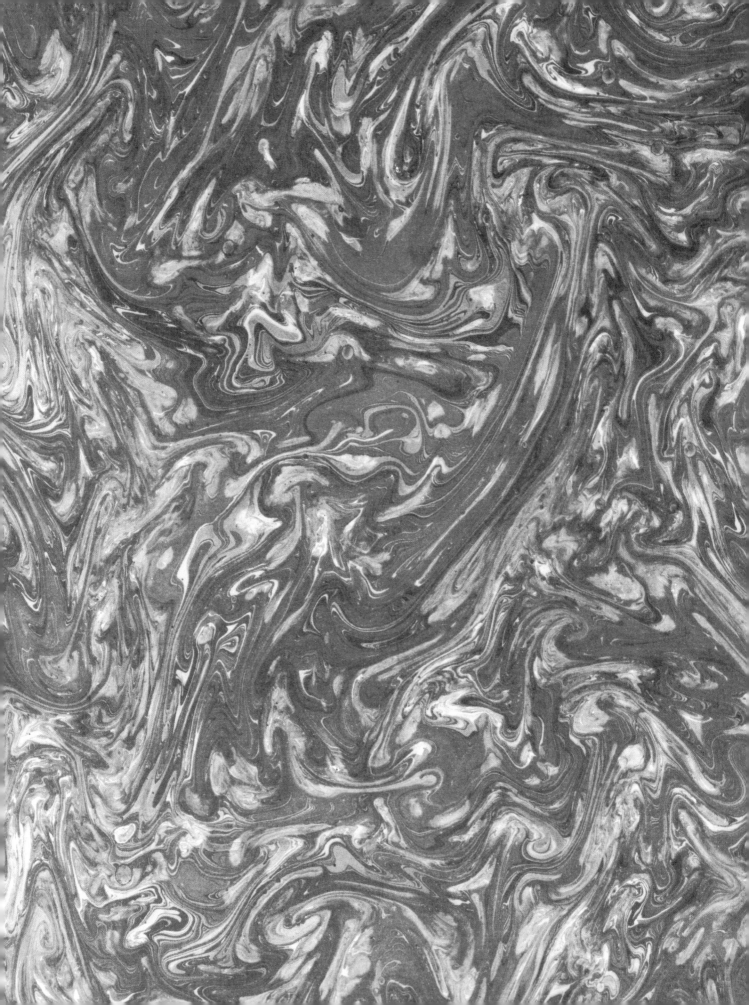

CHAPTER V – The 1930s

SURVIVING THE GREAT DEPRESSION

Entering the 1930s, the Exchange was considered one of the country's most successful businesses, vigorously advertising its products by promoting the nutritional value of citrus.

BEFORE THE BAD TIMES

As the Exchange approached its 40-year milestone, it could – despite the deepening Depression – find reasons to feel confident about the future. By 1930, the grower-owned cooperative was considered one of the biggest and most successful businesses in the country. Under advertising manager W.B. Geissinger, the Exchange continued the full force of its advertising, which reflected the media of the times. One popular advertising means was the use of promotional signs on the thousands of street cars which crisscrossed the nation's cities. And of course, the Exchange sponsored many weekly musical programs on radio, then one of America's favorite evening entertainments.

Sales of fresh fruit continued strong in the early Thirties, helped by the cooperative's sophisticated approach to marketing. The Sunkist name had become the world's best known trademark of fresh fruit. The valuable dealer service men employed by the Exchange made personal calls to retailers to demonstrate the benefits and many uses of citrus fruit. One of their responsibilities was installing attractive displays of fruit to entice buyers. They were also charged with promoting the use of citrus drinks by visiting the nation's thousands of retail outlets. They made sure Sunkist juice extractors and reamers were in as many of these outlets as possible.

The Exchange also had its experienced sales agents in 57 districts into which it had divided the American market. These salaried sales representatives reported to their respective headquarters on a regular basis about all factors that influenced the sale of Exchange fruit. In 1932, manager of the Eastern division was J.O. Cook. The Central division was managed by J.P. Scanlan, the Northern division by S.E. Priest, the Southern division by R.H. James, and the Western division by W.C. McPherson.

General sales manager was T.H. Powell. It was his responsibility to oversee the sale of Exchange fruit, some 45 percent of which was now sold to buyers through public auctions. Most of these auctions took place in major American cities where the buyers were most concentrated.

And, of course, the central Exchange relied on some 25 district exchanges, representing the more than 200 associations affiliated with the cooperative, in the sale of their fruit. Throughout the year, a distribution committee comprised of district exchange managers and representatives of the sales and field departments met each Wednesday to determine the fruit distribution program for the following week.

All sales information was centralized at the Exchange headquarters in Los Angeles. Because speed was essential in marketing a perishable product, the Exchange relied on the teletype, "that marvel of modern communication." Installed in 1930, the teletype relayed late-breaking market news and sales information from salesmen to district ex-

By 1931, The Exchange Orange Products Company at Ontario, California had surpassed the million-dollar mark in the sales of orange by-products such as juice and pectin.

change offices every hour of every day. This Market News Service was not confined to the domestic market. Information to and from foreign markets was also sent.

Export sales had become increasingly important for the Exchange. Only ten years earlier, 50,000 boxes of California citrus fruit were considered a big year's export. In 1931, the Exchange shipped nearly a million boxes of valencia oranges alone to Europe.

Getting that fruit to its destination on time and in good condition was the traffic department's job. It handled rates, refrigeration charges and routings, and made the bookings on steamship lines. It cleared shipments through customs houses and took care of marine insurance. For the Exchange, that involved the annual movement of some 60,000 rail cars of perishable fruit, originating at more than 200 packing houses in widely separated parts of the state. The average haul was about 2,500 miles.

TURNING CULLS INTO PROFITS

There were also increasingly profitable by-products developments to lend optimism to Exchange members. If anything was a marvel, it was how the Exchange had managed to take the fruit which growers once paid to discard and turn it into a profitable commodity. In the early part of the century, growers had been compelled to dump their culled fruit and pay a charge of as much as $2 a ton to do it. Now, development of by-products had turned losses into profits.

In a forward-looking action in the early Thirties, the cooperative's Exchange Lemon By-Products Company, started back in 1915, replaced its old building in Corona with a new steel and concrete structure, "practically fireproof."

The Exchange Orange Products Company in Ontario completed a new, three-story warehouse and remodeled its pectin plant. For the first time in its history, sales of orange by-products had surpassed the million-dollar mark. In fact, the orange by-products business looked so promising, the Exchange had reported, "The problem of the company in 1929-30 was not what to do with its products but how to obtain enough fruit to supply the demands of its customers." By the end of the decade, the Exchange would operate a second orange by-products plant at Lindsay, in the San Joaquin Valley.

The Thirties would see the Exchange ship its first substantial volumes of canned orange juice. This outstanding development had been in the works for several years. Initially, though, opinion had been sharply divided over the long-term benefits to growers. In the long run, of course, the consumer would settle the question of whether it was worthwhile to continue producing canned orange juice.

The Fruit Growers Supply Company was also succeeding admirably. By 1931, its volume of business had reached $10 million. Most of that represented orchard and packinghouse supplies sold to Exchange members. These included boxes, tissue wraps, nails, fertilizers, orchard heaters, oil, and equipment. By 1932, the Supply Company required over 100 million board feet of lumber annually for the making of Exchange box shook.

BACKED BY GROWER BELIEF

By 1932, the Exchange was made up of more than 13,000 citrus fruit growers, producing more than 75 percent of the California citrus crop. In fact, three out of every four California citrus growers were members of the Exchange. And Arizona now had a representative on the Exchange board: F.W. Avery, president of Arizona Citrus Growers, a 370-member association which operated packing plants in Phoenix and in Mesa.

The heavy volume – 25 million boxes of fruit – shipped by the Exchange each year allowed marketing costs to be kept low. And the smoothly-functioning cooperative was returning $75-$100 million a year to members.

It wasn't just the consistently higher results members received from the Exchange that earned their support. According to a 1932 publication from the Exchange, growers believed in the Exchange because they were convinced of its integrity and fairness.

Twenty-six directors – each a grower – sat on the Board, and also formed the directorate of the Fruit Growers Supply Company and The Exchange Orange Products Company. Each director was an elected representative from a district exchange, which consisted of numerous packing associations, owned and operated by the growers themselves.

In fact, there were over 200 packinghouse associations in the Exchange system, each considered a fundamental unit. Their role was to harvest the fruit of members, prepare it for market under strict grading standards, and load it on rail cars. Each association had its own brand names to identify to the trade the quality of its own local fruit. The associations were the units which received from the Exchange the returns for all fruit shipped, minus the actual cost of the central and district organizations. This money was then distributed – after packinghouse costs had been deducted – to the association's members in proportion to each grower's volume and quality.

This multi-level form of representation assured grower control and management of the Exchange. Each Exchange director had one vote, "because neither capital nor the volume of business contributed is the infallible measure of a man's fairness and judgment," The Sunkist Courier reported. They discussed the matters of the Exchange every week.

"Nothing is covered up," noted a 1932 Exchange publication. "Its business policy is determined at weekly open meetings of its grower-directors, meetings which any grower may attend. Each of its associations and its district exchanges every day receive hourly a record of all of the sales of fruit which the Exchange makes, the markets where sold, the prices received on each size of each grade, and even a transcript of the telegraphic negotiations preceding the sales which were exchanged between the central office in California and the office in the market where sold."

Named general manager in 1931, Paul S. Armstrong held that position for 25 years.

ARMSTRONG BECOMES PRESIDENT

And, as the Thirties opened, there was another reason to look forward with confidence. A new hand would now be guiding the day-to-day operations of the Exchange. It belonged to Paul S. Armstrong.

Armstrong was named general manager in August 1931. His selection by the board of directors had been made after Dezell's death, which had been considered a severe loss. Not only manager of the Exchange for almost 10 years, Dezell had been employed by the organization since 1897. But the cigar-smoking Armstrong, who had joined the Exchange in 1916 and had worked closely with Dezell for several years, was prepared to assume the duties of the general manager – or chief executive officer – of the Exchange. It was a position he would hold for 25 years.

Armstrong's appointment to the Exchange's top management post did not come without cost. Company folklore holds that orange sales manager Dana King had also been a contender for the general manager position. King had been connected with the Exchange since 1903, and had devised the modern district sales office system under which the organization's sales operated. It is said that King resigned the day Armstrong was appointed general manager. Deeply regretful of his departure, the board of directors felt compelled to honor him with these words, "Mr. King has served Exchange growers long and faithfully. Much of his life has been translated into the life and prosperity of the organization, so intimate and personal has been his interest in the task that was his. It follows naturally that he is universally beloved and that his influence is wide and will long continue."

The position of chief executive officer had always been a challenging one in the Exchange. Now, Armstrong would have a challenging era to go along with it.

THE GREAT DEPRESSION

As the Thirties progressed, the Great Depression intensified. Business failed. Banks closed. Unemployment ran rampant. The dust bowl of Oklahoma, Kansas, Texas and other parched states had sent thousands of farmers and other displaced people off to California to look for work. By the third year of the decade, even California's previously insulated citrus growers were feeling the adverse affects of the nation's Depression. Nineteen thirty-three was "an unprecedented one in all lines of business," the Exchange reported, and "only lemons made a compensatory return per acre to the grower."

Previously, citrus had maintained a relatively better position than most other lines of agriculture and industry. Consumer demand for citrus fruit had held up remarkably well under the nation's widespread unemployment and financial distress. But by 1933, citrus prices had fallen to or below the cost of production.

Despite the devastation of the Depression years, the Exchange did not slow its shipments, but continued to offer normal volumes.

Exchange citrus shipments hit rough roads with the unusual complications presented by the banking situation across the country. As uneasiness grew in business and financial circles, wholesalers began to tighten up on credits, often refusing to sell to even old customers except on a cash basis. By March 6, 1933, all banks in the U.S. were closed on order of the federal government. Restrictions were partially lifted a week later, and more fully in following days, but in some of the country's largest population centers, enormous sums of money continued to be tied up in closed and restricted banks.

The Exchange decided that rather than stop or slow its shipments, it would continue to offer its normal volumes. To operate under the uncertain atmosphere, the Exchange extended additional credit to the trade. Auctions were also requested to extend credit to responsible buyers even though remittances to California would be delayed. "It seemed better to take the risk than permit the fruit to remain, and probably waste, in California, for sales lost with a perishable commodity are never regained," the Exchange reported.

The cooperative took another step to weather the Depression by cutting the salaries of its 467 employees 10 percent across the board in 1933. It began to utilize air mail to a greater extent in place of telegrams. A teletypewriter service was installed between the Los Angeles headquarters and certain sales offices.

GROWERS STRUGGLE

Out in their citrus groves, growers also were struggling with their own immediate problems of survival. Probably most pressing was their inability to depend on their local banks for short-term seasonal financing or long-term mortgage financing of their operations.

The U.S. government – under President Franklin D. Roosevelt's New Deal – sought to lift America out of its Depression. In a move to help the nation's farmers, the Farm Credit Act of 1933 was made into law. This established Production Credit Associations to lend farmers money for production expenses.

As other ways were sought to bring profitability back to the nation's farming industry, a major policy with long-term ramifications was created. On May 12, 1933 the Agricultural Adjustment Act was passed into law. One of its objectives was to "seek to adjust supply to demand and compel all producers or handlers in an industry to assume their fair share of market regulation and, when necessary, of surplus control," the Exchange reported.

The Exchange viewed this legislation as vitally important to the economic well-being of the California-Arizona citrus industry. "It is significant that these plans, induced by the national emergency, closely parallel the voluntary efforts and methods which Exchange growers have been using for some years past in the handling of their own business," the cooperative noted in its 1933 annual report.

As early as 1923, in an endeavor to improve unsatisfactory price levels through proration of shipments, the Exchange had established an informal distribution committee. In

1925, a formal agreement for lemons had been entered into by Exchange lemon shippers representing about 90 percent of the entire California crop, specifying that lemon shipments would be controlled under prorates. This agreement was, the Exchange said in 1933, "the means of which the lemon industry has successfully handled a burdensome surplus situation for the past eight years, [and] is generally recognized as a milestone in cooperative progress."

Although the new legislation had its opponents, citrus growers in California, Florida and Texas adopted separate but similar provisions to put a marketing plan into place, one that created a balance between supply and demand and produced market stability. In the Far West, where 82 percent of the industry had declared itself for prorate, an industry committee called the California-Arizona Orange Grapefruit Committee worked with both the U.S. Secretary of Agriculture and the California State Director of Agriculture to operate a volume-regulated shipping program.

In the midst of these changes, the Exchange took time to divert its thinking from prorate to honor one of its own. In 1933, "in recognition of the splendid character of services rendered, W.E. Sprott, first vice president of the Exchange, upon retiring from the board on September 1 at the age of 78 years, was appointed honorary vice president," the Exchange proclaimed. Sprott had represented the growers of the Tulare County Fruit Exchange on the Exchange board for 29 years. It was only the second time an honorary officer had been named in the 40-year history of the Exchange – F.Q. Story being the first.

Despite the deepening troubles of the Depression, the Exchange continued with full force its research and development programs. By 1933, it directly owned The Exchange Orange Products Company at Ontario. Exchange advertising continued to promote the Sunkist name, to build consumer demand and to encourage a variety of uses for citrus. During the 1934-35 season, the Exchange invested over $2 million in advertising, promoting the Sunkist name and its high-quality citrus in magazines, newspapers – including color pages in Sunday editions – street car cards, posters, neonized paint signs, and of course, on radio spots. Since the first big 1907 campaign, the Exchange had spent almost $22 million on advertising.

Surveys indicated that advertising by the Exchange had played a big role in increasing per-capita consumption of oranges from just 31 a year in 1906, to 52 by 1926, to 79 by 1936. In 1939, the Exchange became the first Western advertiser to win first prize in the national outdoor advertising art exhibit. The winner was a Sunkist cold lemonade poster.

THE EXCHANGE MAKES A MOVE

Careful management through the difficult Depression years kept the Exchange financially strong. This allowed the Exchange to decide upon a rather drastic move in 1934, when all around it, businesses were failing.

With the lease on the Consolidated Building at Sixth and Hill Streets about to expire, Exchange directors and management evaluated their office arrangements. Since 1893, Exchange headquarters had been in rented facilities. Conscious of saving the grower-member as much money as possible, Exchange directors decided to capitalize on depressed property values to purchase a permanent property site for the Exchange. By constructing its own building, the Exchange could save a substantial sum each year on money that would have been spent on renting office space.

Constructed of reinforced concrete frames and floor systems, the Sunkist Building was designed "as probably the first Class 'A' office structure in Los Angeles."

Built in 1935, the Sunkist Building stood seven floors tall and exceeded earthquake requirements of the day. The exterior facade was embellished with low-relief sculptured panels.

Huge colorful murals of early California citrus scenes adorned the board room walls in the new Sunkist Building. The paintings hang today in the board room of Sunkist headquarters in Sherman Oaks.

A piece of property was acquired for $117,000 at Fifth and Hope Streets in downtown Los Angeles, directly across the street from the Los Angeles Public Library. Detailed plans for a building were developed. The new structure would cost $365,000. Construction began in the spring of 1934. Both the property and the building were financed under extremely low interest rates. By late 1935, the new Sunkist building was ready for its occupants, "a source of joy and pride to every one who works in it," the Exchange reported. Seven stories tall, the new building housed a much-needed auditorium for the heavily-attended weekly meetings of directors and growers. There was even a diet kitchen and laboratory for research.

Its architect, Robert Field, said the Sunkist Building was the first office building in the center of a major city to have poured concrete walls and detailed enrichment. And it was earthquake-proof.

Huge colorful murals adorned the board room at the 707 West Fifth Street building. The work of Frank Bowers and Arthur Prunier, the murals depicted historical California citrus scenes. They showed the introduction of the orange into the area by the Spanish padres, and men, women and children engaged in the harvesting and packing of citrus fruit.

MAKING THE BEST OF A BAD SITUATION

Exchange expenses for operating and advertising were curtailed following a severe freeze in January 1937 that left 40 percent of the citrus fruit on the trees unfit for shipment. That loss amounted to 16 million boxes, or 35,000 carloads. The problem of segregating the good fruit from the bad was tremendous. The biggest burden fell on packinghouse managers and workers.

But they found help in an innovation that arrived that year. A new X-ray sorting machine had been developed by the General Electric Corporation in collaboration with the Exchange's field department. The machine used fluoroscopic methods to reveal the fruit's interior quality without cutting the peel. After the freeze, some 73 X-ray machines were used in 57 Exchange packinghouses to inspect over 3.25 million boxes of fruit, out of which 2 million packed boxes were salvaged and sold as fresh fruit.

As another way of expanding its markets, the Exchange helped develop an arrangement with Western Union and Postal Telegraph in 1937 for delivering Christmas gifts of Sunkist oranges throughout the United States.

Still, by 1938, the rule rather than exception across America was one of bountiful harvests and accompanying low prices. During the 1938-39 season, America's citrus groves set a new production record of 135 million boxes of oranges, lemons and grapefruit. The sharpest production increase was seen in Florida and Texas. With surplus production

TEN ADVANTAGES TO CITRUS GROWERS
OF A LARGER EXCHANGE MEMBERSHIP

1.
More orderly regulation of the total volume of shipments.

2.
More systematic distribution of shipments among the markets.

3.
A larger fund for consumer advertising and trade work
to develop additional demand and open new markets.

4.
More complete and accurate records of the
consuming capacity of all the markets at all times.

5.
A better and more equitable handling
of emergency conditions in the industry.

6.
A broader use of improvements in cultural and packing methods.

7.
Lower marketing costs.

8.
Lower cost of supplies.

9.
More trade confidence in the stability of the market.

10.
A stronger unified position for the industry in handling
freight rates, tariffs and every problem common to all growers.

"All these benefits result in a higher net return to the Grower."

from the 1932 annual report of the
California Fruit Growers Exchange

and reduced consumer buying power, navel oranges averaged only $1.44 per box, (F.O.B. Calif.) compared to the previous year's already-slim $1.46. Many growers could not even cover the expenses of producing their crops. In the citrus industry, as always, the biggest fixed item of expense was freight.

"In the case of California oranges, for example," the Exchange reported in late 1938, "the freight charge per box this year exceeded the gross return to the grower who produced the fruit. No one can be unmindful of the financial problems of the railroads in this difficult times, but in their own interest as well as that of the citrus industry which depends on them for transportation to market, they must devise some means of performing this essential service at a lower cost or the traffic itself will disappear."

THE TENSION OVER PRORATE

Against this background, a bitter battle was growing between the Exchange and independent shippers. The Exchange advocated proration – the orderly distribution of fruit. It had voluntarily operated under such a concept since the Twenties. And orderly distribution – one of the cooperative's cornerstones from its very beginning – was becoming even more necessary with the explosion of citrus production.

"It is my firm conviction, after much experience and study of the problem of marketing for many years," Exchange president Teague wrote years later, "that if the citrus industry had not first enjoyed the benefit of proration set up by the Exchange, and later the enforced proration established by state and federal legislation, it would have been in much the same demoralized condition that characterized it during the early Nineties."

The greatly expanded plantings of citrus trees during the boom times of the Twenties were now resulting in larger and larger crops. In fact, California's 1935 lemon crop had been 69 percent larger in volume than the greatest sales ever made. Even though the Exchange handled 90 percent of the state's lemons, this dramatic increase was too much for one handler alone to effectively – or fairly – regulate.

Experience had shown the Exchange that supply and demand could be expected to be out of balance in some seasons. By having a carefully regulated distribution of citrus shipments, gluts and shortages – and the resulting price swings – could be prevented. The cooperative believed that orderly marketing benefited not only the producer but the trade and the consumer as well.

Yet some growers chafed under the new regulations, which required them to delegate to government agencies a certain amount of authority. There were restrictions on their individual freedom in determining when their crops were harvested and shipped. Still, the Exchange maintained that the prorate regulations secured the greatest possible returns and allowed all growers – not just its 14,000 members – to share equitably in the marketing opportunities.

The situation was further aggravated by the extremely large crops and the low buying power of the public. Non-Exchange shippers vigorously opposed the prorate policy and attacked the constitutionality of the marketing order statute. They said the entire crop could be marketed profitably without prorate. Among growers, there was a lack of understanding about the regulations.

"There is a constant temptation under the stress of these conditions to depart from sound marketing practices, a tendency which is encouraged and promoted by those who profit by disorganization in an industry," the Exchange cautioned.

On November 10, 1938, the eight-member industry distribution committee failed to set a prorate on orange shipments for the coming week. The four industry members from the Mutual Orange Distributors and the American Fruit Growers had succeeded in blocking the prorate decision.

TEAGUE'S RADIO TALKS

To counter the spread of misinformation about prorate, Exchange president Teague made a series of ten radio talks – at his own expense – between Nov. 22 and Dec. 15, 1938.

"Prorate makes it possible to ship a thousand cars of oranges this week and a thousand cars next week at stable prices, instead of fifteen hundred cars this week and five hundred cars next week at red-ink prices," Teague explained in his November 22 broadcast.

"Proration cannot succeed on a hit or miss basis," Teague told his audience. "So long as a small and admittedly antagonistic minority has the power to upset it, we must be on guard."

On November 29, Teague urged, "Fellow growers, our two immediate needs are proration and the expansion of consumer demand. The means of getting this expansion are already set up in the industry's great, grower-owned cooperative."

Watching from the sidelines, *The Los Angeles* Times reported on December 5, 1938, "For years, the Exchange has kept quiet under constant sniping by its smaller rivals. It has turned the other cheek till there is no cheek left to turn. Now, for a change, it is showing a few teeth. . . As head of an organization representing 75 percent of the industry and sponsor of a marketing system that benefits 100 percent of it, [President Teague] has a right to warn obstructers that further interference with orderly marketing methods will not be tolerated. . . .

"Prorating and advertising have been the twin foundation stones of the industry's success," the newspaper continued. "The Exchange has carried the burden in both programs. . . The Exchange is doing the grower, the shipper and the consumer a favor by detailing the facts and pointing the remedy."

"Results of [President Teague's broadcasts] were not unlike the first shot at Lexington," the *Pacific Rural Press* reported on December 24, 1938. "Citrus growers jumped into the fray. Public sentiment crystallized rapidly and the marketing agreement was quickly restored. . . . And what started out as an old-fashioned revival of cooperative spirit among citrus growers, has spread into other groups, and history is being made."

The response to Teague's talks was overwhelming. He received hundreds of telegrams and letters supporting his efforts. One of them, from the Riverside Arlington Heights Fruit Exchange, typified the response.

"Outside shippers now declare themselves for the prorate Stop," the telegram said. "There is a reason and you are it Stop Congratulations Stop We urge you to continue your series of broadcasts to completion, our competitors attitude probably temporary and expedient. All growers are receiving an Exchange education and they like it."

Backed by the majority of growers, the Exchange's philosophy had prevailed. But the problems of the nation's depressed economy lingered. Everyone looked for a recovery of some kind. Government programs designed to assist rural America helped to some extent. But they were not enough. The recovery of the nation's economy held particular significance for the citrus industry, since it could not prosper unless buying power was widespread and consumers enjoyed a decent standard of living. And in California, the fate of the citrus industry was no small matter. In the late Thirties, it was second only to oil in importance to the prosperity of the state. The citrus industry brought in over $100 million a year to California, and at least 200,000 people derived their livelihood directly from it.

The ultimate cure for the Great Depression was a long time coming, although only a few Americans realized it when it actually began. In 1939, a cataclysmic world war was brewing thousands of miles away that would finally but painfully wrench America out of its economic misery.

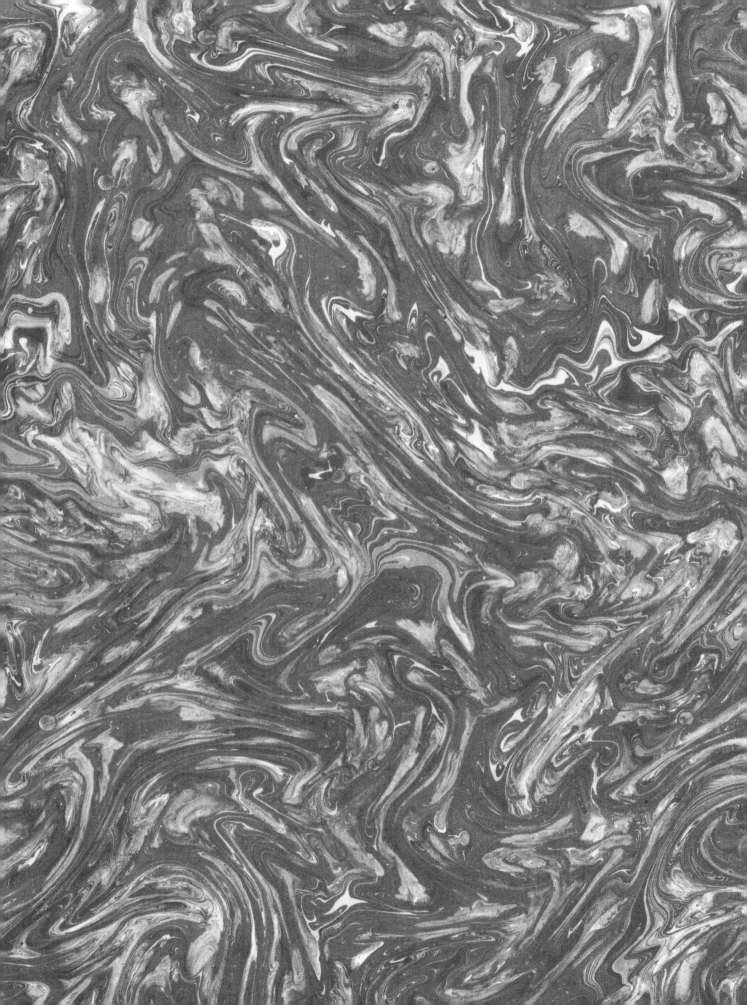

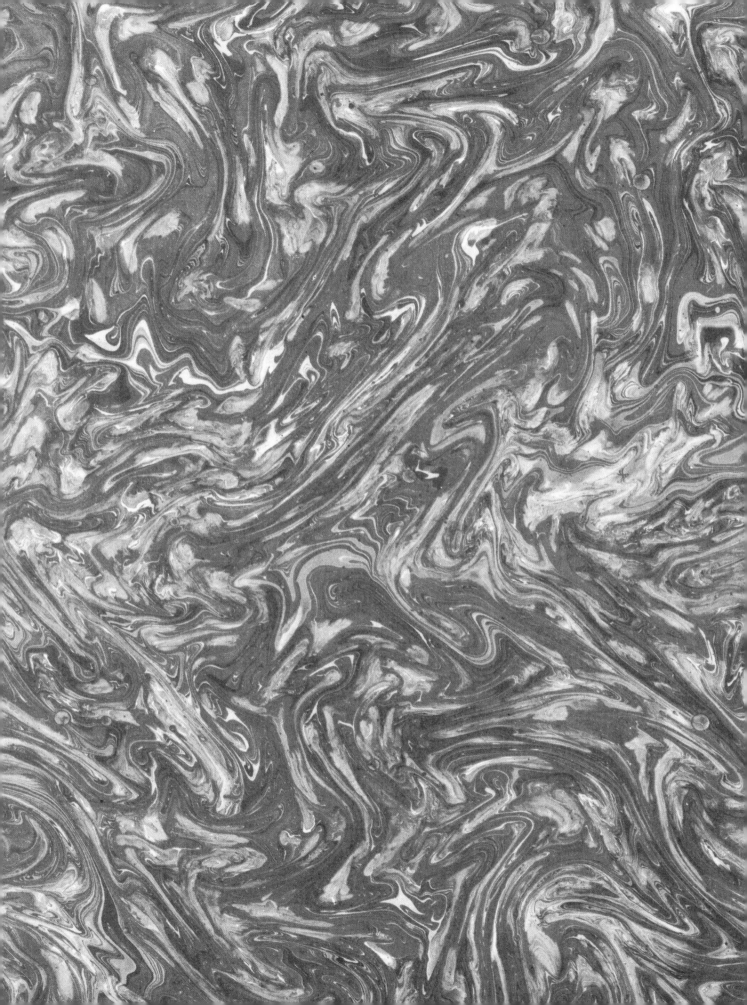

CHAPTER VI – The 1940s

THE WAR YEARS

In greeting Yoeman Fred W. Leggitt, Jr., a Sunkist employee who enlisted in the navy during World War II, President C.C. Teague saluted all 44 California Fruit Growers Exchange employees then serving in the armed forces.

THE EXCHANGE AND THE WAR EFFORT

For America – and the California Fruit Growers Exchange – the world changed overnight after the Japanese attack on Pearl Harbor on December 7, 1941.

The War Effort would become the driving force in the minds of Americans at home. Doing its part, the Exchange went to work, supplying the fighting forces of America and its allies with a food supply deemed a strategic commodity.

Initially, it had been the "War in Europe," which had occupied the minds of Americans. Its impact had not yet been acute, although it had closed some increasingly important markets for the Exchange. After Hitler invaded Poland in 1939, tensions had escalated quickly. In 1940, with the Blitz terrorizing England, the London sales office of the Exchange had been closed. All shipments were terminated. The loss of an important annual outlet for Exchange fruit had placed an added burden on the already complex marketing problem of the largest California citrus crop.

But as the War intensified, demand for fresh oranges and lemons, as well as citrus concentrates, increased sharply. In fact, by 1943, demand exceeded supply most of the time. This was made all the more astounding because the national grapefruit crop that season was the biggest ever, while the lemon crop was the second largest on record.

"We are living in a war economy," general manager Armstrong reported in late 1941, "the duration of which and the final result of which are not known to anyone. . . . The citrus industry is an important provider of protective foods; and every effort should be made to maintain an adequate production of good quality, handled and distributed with skill and efficiency. . . . It is to be hoped that during this period the citrus industry may improve its relative economic position, which had not been at all comfortable during the depression years."

Armstrong's words were prophetic. The citrus industry did improve its "relative economic position," enough so that by the next next year, Armstrong could open his 1942 annual report with optimism.

"During a year in which the distribution of most products was drastically affected by the world war and many businesses were completely transformed to the war effort or abandoned," Armstrong reported, "the Exchange, with its health-promoting fruit and fruit products, found itself in a relatively encouraging position. The citrus industry is recognized as an essential industry. The products which it has to market are needed in the war effort and greatly needed. . . . What problems citrus growers face as the war continues, none can completely foresee; but whatever they may be, the industry is better off than most. It still has something to sell; something the Government wants sold; something that is vital to the winning of the war."

Armstrong added, "What specifically is the Exchange doing today to help win the war? For that must be, and is, the primary objective for the duration."

To meet military requests for specific grades and sizes of fresh fruit on demand, the Exchange established an Army and Navy pool arrangement where the citrus could be supplied on very short notice. One of the cooperative's biggest contributions to the War Effort came from its Exchange Products Companies. The two plants – lemon by-products at Corona, orange by-products at Ontario – had been working day and night since Pearl Harbor. Millions of gallons of citrus concentrates were being produced by these Exchange Products Companies. Over 65 percent of their output was filling government orders. The products were shipped to Russia, to England, and of course, to American and Allied soldiers fighting overseas.

By the 1940s, the Exchange's by-products divisions were producing more than 75 percent of all the lemon oil in the U.S., and 45 percent of the orange oil. They also made juice products, pectin and citric acid. Operations for these by-products as well as fresh fruit flourished during World War II as unprecedented wartime demand stimulated the need for citrus products.

Early in 1942, the Exchange completed a new utility building for its Orange Products Company. In August, the Exchange had a large additional stainless steel evaporating pan, a third 250 HP boiler, cooling tower, and new electric power facilities – all needed if the maximum amount of concentrated orange juice was to be made from available fruit.

In 1942, over 320,000 gallons of straight orange juice and 800,000 gallons of concentrated orange juice made by or for the Exchange orange products plant went to the armed forces at home or abroad or for the government-sponsored Lend-Lease Program. Substantial quantities of lemon juice were also furnished. Some half million pounds of pectin produced by the Exchange orange and lemon by-products plants were provided for government use.

Much of the Lend-Lease shipments went to a beleaguered England, which had been at war with Germany since 1939. When the Exchange's fresh oranges and lemons arrived in England, they were often offered in contests as prizes to civilians, many of whom had not seen such fruit since the start of the War.

Over 10,000 carloads of Exchange citrus were shipped in concentrated form under the Lend-Lease Program during 1943 – the year of cooperative's 50th anniversary. That was twice the amount that had been exported annually before the War. It was an ongoing source of pride to the Exchange that its research and development over the many years made it possible for its products to reach soldiers and nations thousands of miles away.

At home, thousands of commercial juice extractors were sold by the Exchange to government agencies to make fresh citrus juice available to America's fighting forces. In fact,

Testing the firmness of pectin – a major product in jelly-making – at the Exchange's Orange Products Lab in Ontario.   Inset: Barrels of dried pectin are prepared for shipment to England under the U.S. Lend-Lease Program of World War II.

Top left: Following Pearl Harbor, the Exchanges' two by-products plants worked day and night with more than 65% of their output filling government orders.   Top right: Operations for citrus by-products as well as fresh fruit flourished during World War II as unprecedented war time demand stimulated the need for citrus products.   Bottom left: The Exchange sold thousands of commercial juice extractors like these during World War II to provide America's soldiers with fresh citrus juice.   Bottom right: During World War II, the Exchange Products Companies produced millions of gallons of citrus concentrates, mixing them in cold wall tanks. Much of the concentrates were consumed through the Lend-Lease Program.

the U.S. government became the largest customer of citrus concentrates, purchasing millions of gallons of orange, lemon and grapefruit juices for the Lend-Lease Program.

In 1944, the War Food Administration Achievement "A" flag was presented to the employees of The Exchange Orange Products Company in recognition of their contribution to the War food program. It was the first Southern California plant to receive the award.

The Exchange also backed the War Effort on a far more personal scale. Just two months after the Pearl Harbor attack, the Exchange already had 27 employees serving in the armed forces of the U.S. or Canada. Dozens of employees donated to the Red Cross blood bank. By 1942, over 80 employees had entered military service, and all of them had assurances that jobs awaited them upon their return.

COPING WITH SHORTAGES

As the War progressed, the Exchange and its packinghouses faced labor shortages which created "serious and persistent" problems. "Great credit is due to the packinghouse managers and foremen for their resourcefulness in conducting their operations in the face of most difficult and unusual conditions," the Exchange noted in late 1943.

Through the Exchange, the services of thousands of Mexican nationals were used to help harvest the citrus crops through the War years.

Manpower wasn't the only commodity in short supply. The vast requirements of the War Effort for lumber and other forest products made wood one of the most critical war materials. With the unprecedented demand and record crops, boxes were critically scarce. By 1945, the California-Arizona citrus industry was using about 200 million board feet of lumber a year for boxes. That year, too, the California-Arizona citrus industry set an all-time shipping record of 140,544 cars of fresh fruit.

During this time, the Supply Company made its third purchase of timberland, buying land in Shasta County and acquiring cutting rights on additional timber in Lassen and Plumas counties. It also obtained a mill operation at Westwood, California.

"Had it not been for the Fruit Growers Supply Company, owned by growers," Armstrong noted in 1945, "part of the crop could not have been shipped this year for want of containers."

BUILDING CONSUMER DEMAND

Although the War in the European and Pacific theaters was foremost in everyone's minds, the Exchange continued to direct efforts to build consumer demand at home. The cooperative's dealer service campaign remained in full force during the 1941-42 season, with 55 men on staff to call on fresh fruit and extractor outlets across the nation. They also installed thousands of citrus-promoting displays in retail and wholesale stores.

Through the War years, women in Exchange packinghouses handled record crops of oranges and lemons. These gloved packers are filling each box with oranges of uniform size.

SUNKIST MAKING HISTORY

1893
Some 100 orange growers organize a marketing cooperative to sell and distribute their fruit.

1894
Southern California Fruit Exchange formally opened in Los Angeles.

1905
California Fruit Growers Exchange incorporated as a cooperative.

1907-08
Organization becomes first farmer group to advertise a perishable product
in a national campaign.

1907
First use of Sunkist trademark for citrus fruit.

1909
Sunkist trademark registered.

1910
First inspector employed to check quality of fruit.

1915
Sunkist products division begins with a small marmalade factory.

1916
Sunkist first to promote orange juice, with the "Drink An Orange" campaign.

1916
Sunkist first food group to offer a premium with its fruits, with the
"Orange Blossom" silverware offer.

1922
Sunkist first to use the word "vitamine" (Vitamin C) in its advertising.

1926
Sunkist trademark first successfully stamped on fresh oranges.

Late 1920s
Sunkist sponsors the first-ever commercial radio broadcasts between California
and the East Coast; the first company to use motion picture stars on radio.

1944
First company in Southern California, and the second in the state, to be awarded the War
Food Administration's coveted "A" flag in recognition of outstanding achievement in the
production of essential food. Presented to The Exchange Orange Products Company,
forerunner of Sunkist's orange products division.

1952
Company name changes to Sunkist from California Fruit Growers Exchange.

1977
Sunkist licenses its trademark for the bottling and marketing of Sunkist orange soda.

1990
Total Sunkist revenues top $1 billion in a single year.

1993
Believed to be the first U.S. agricultural cooperative to reach 100 consecutive years of business.

To kick off the Treasury Department's 1941 campaign to sell Defense stamps and bonds, the National Association of Retail Grocers installed a booth at the Mayflower Hotel in Washington, D.C. Prominent among labels was the Sunkist name. At far right is Alexander Smith, Sunkist dealer service representative.   Inset: Ration stamps during World War II could be used to buy Sunkist oranges.

That year, too, the Exchange helped launch a drive to ensure that 150 California schools provided fresh orange juice to their students. In fact, educational materials had been distributed to schools by the Exchange since the Twenties. In 1940, the cooperative circulated two films to schools, "Citrus On Parade," and "The Golden Journey."

The Exchange continued to use its research and laboratory to test many products that might be of value to the industry, such as products for decay control, algae control, treated wrappers, water treatments for the elimination of scale deposits, brine treatment, corrosion-resisting compounds, soaps, label pastes, and waxes.

Part of the demand for citrus was propelled not only by the War Effort but a much publicized national defense movement for better diets for American families. It called for Americans to "Get Your Vitamins The Natural Way." The Exchange capitalized on the crusade by intensifying its advertising.

In 1940, the Exchange used network radio – coast-to-coast broadcasting – to advertise its Sunkist brand name. Airing on "Hedda Hopper's Hollywood," the Exchange-sponsored program ran three times a week, 15 minutes per broadcast, on 39 Columbia Broadcasting Stations throughout the year. "The use of key CBS stations in the larger centers insured good coverage of these populous markets and at the same time wide coverage of the surrounding rural and small town territory, thus covering by radio most of the principal consuming areas of the nation throughout the year," the Exchange reported.

During the 1941-42 season, with Teague as Exchange president, member-growers were investing in their advertising program 7 cents per packed box of oranges and 12 cents on lemons. The cooperative bombarded national newspapers, magazines like the *Saturday Evening Post*, and radio with advertisements. It placed posters in key locations – like New York subways – with advertisements proclaiming "Citrus Fruits for Health."

In one of the most popular pieces in its advertising history, the Exchange promoted the "Sunkist Baby" in its valencia orange advertisements. The healthy little girl showed, in consecutive ads, how nicely "Sunkist-fed" babies grew from year to year.

Just as importantly, the Exchange used its advertisements to explain the vital role of oranges and lemons in the War Effort, and that California citrus growers were producers of these essential foods.

The Exchange backed its advertising with its cornerstone commitment to quality. "Quality is remembered long after price is forgotten," *The Sunkist Courier* reported in early 1942.

1943: A HALF-CENTURY MILESTONE

The Exchange celebrated its half-century anniversary in 1943, proudly remembering how it had been "soundly conceived and soundly built."

"The Exchange is an industrial democracy securing for its members the tremendous resources of cooperative action and yet carefully preserving for the individual the rewards of his own skill in production," the cooperative asserted.

With almost 14,600 members, the Exchange represented 75 percent of the orange, lemon and grapefruit growers in California and Arizona in 1943. That year, it honored seven loyal growers who continuously had been members of the cooperative since its inception in 1893. They were: Fred J. Smith, Mrs. J.G. Robertson, and Mrs. J.E. Adamson of Pomona Fruit Growers Exchange; Chauncey S. Sheldon of La Verne Orange Association; Edmund C. Robinson of Indian Hill Citrus Association; James Mills, Sr. of James Mills Orchards Corporation; and Mrs. C.C. Warren of Glendora Citrus Association.

By 1943, there were 200 local packinghouses feeding into 25 local District Exchanges of the cooperative's marketing network. In its 50th year, the Exchange would pack more than 37 million boxes of oranges, lemons and grapefruit. In fact, the cooperative would contribute more to America's armed forces and allies alone than it had supplied to the entire nation during that initial year of 1893.

PRICE CONTROL DIFFERENCES

During the War years, a price control program was placed by the Office of Price Administration on several important food commodities, the first being the American citrus crop. "The industry is in favor of the necessary steps that must be taken from time to time to prevent inflation during the war period," the Exchange reported, "and has every desire to cooperate fully in this regard on any program which is sound in operation and equitable in its result."

By 1943, however, an unpopular price ceiling dictated that the maximum price for California and Arizona oranges was $3.43 per box, F.O.B. For grapefruit, it was $2.28 per box, F.O.B. The price restrictions did not take into account, the Exchange believed, the rapid increases in production and handling costs occasioned by the rapid advance in the cost of labor and essential materials. Because it was difficult to fairly establish and effectively enforce rigid price controls on perishable commodities, the program was "neither satisfactory to the industry nor to the government," the Exchange reported.

What made the situation so critical was that the government was such a large customer of the Exchange, the cooperative often found it impossible to supply the volume of fruit for the by-products demanded by consumers. Yet no one could deny the power and value of this demand for orange juice and concentrates. In January 1943, a federal order was issued, directing every orange shipper to "set aside" a quantity of oranges each week equivalent to 20 percent of his fresh fruit shipments. "This set-aside order resulted in a well regulated, fairly steady flow of fruit to all producers of concentrated orange juice."

The gross receipts to the Exchange in 1943 from government sales of orange by-products reached over $5.5 million dollars out of a total $7.25 million. Sales from both orange and lemon by-products – all made from fruit once considered a waste – brought in $13 million that season. In early 1944, the Office of Price Administration brought suit against the Exchange and others to recover damages for what it interpreted as a "price ceiling violation." Since the program's beginning, the Exchange and other cooperatives had operated under the belief that cooperative marketing groups had the right to add their selling costs to the established price ceiling in the same manner as other marketers.

In 1944, citrus price ceilings were adjusted to bring slightly increased returns to the grower. And the OPA suit was dismissed by the government.

By 1943, the Exchange marketed its products through 57 Sunkist sales offices. The southern division of the Exchange, managed by R.H. James, spanned 2 million square miles, from North Carolina to Texas. Its central division was headquartered in Chicago. Together, the representatives of these offices worked to deliver fresh fruit to the jobbers and retail store buyers, who in turn filled the orders of more than 500,000 retail fresh fruit dealers, hotels, restaurants, hospitals and other institutions.

One of the Exchange's overseas sales agents, Manila district manager Bob Dameron, was held as a Japanese prisoner-of-war for three years. When finally released, he was given back pay for the duration of his captivity and resumed work with Sunkist's Hawaii office.

SUPPLY GROWS AS THE WAR WINDS DOWN

Citrus production had increased steadily throughout the War years. During the 1944-45 season, citrus production reached an all-time high, with volume peaking at 165 million cartons. In 1944 and 1945, the citrus industry saw peak shipping years.

"It is fortunate for everyone that this record crop was produced in a year when food was greatly needed," the Exchange reported in late 1945.

By the time the War ended in 1945, everyone was ready to get back to peacetime business. After three years of price regulations, the Exchange was glad to see price controls suspended in late 1945. "Our distribution has been distorted by the war economy, particularly by price control," Armstrong wrote. "A return to a free competitive market and more normal marketing practices will be a wholesome thing for the industry."

The close of the War brought quick cancellations of many government orders, making it possible for many of the Exchange by-products to move into civilian channels. By the end of 1945, the Products Department, which handled the sales of both The Exchange Orange Products Company and the Exchange Lemon Products Company, reported total sales at a whopping $11 million. By-products had become such big business, The Exchange Orange Products Company now had a plant at Tempe, Arizona.

Abundant citrus crops continued to record all-time highs. California F.O.B. prices for fresh fruit reflected the effect of the bumper crops. Oranges averaged $4.49 per box during

The 1949 freeze across the citrus-growing areas of California and Arizona matched the benchmark severity of the 1913 and 1937 freezes.

the 1945-46 season; they dropped to just $3.23 the next year. As the decade wound down, prices began to drop below grower's production costs.

The War economy had demonstrated that the basic desire for citrus fruit was great. "Otherwise the huge crops of recent years could not have been marketed," Armstrong reported in 1946.

Widespread buying power was building as America's post-war boom began providing the country's citizens one of the highest standards of living the nation was ever to know. Soldiers were returning home, eager to begin careers and families.

ON THE BRINK OF A NEW ERA

While America stood on the brink of a new era, the citrus industry of Southern California was about to embark on a major transformation. Armstrong could already see it happening in 1947.

"The rapid and persistent growth of Southern California during the war and since is changing somewhat the map of citrus production," the Exchange general manager wrote. "Citrus groves in the Los Angeles Metropolitan area and around the perimeter of the principal citrus belt communities are giving way to sub-division and other types of construction caused by the industrial development in the area. These developments are not only affecting acreage to an appreciable extent (1800 this year), but also bring changes in labor supply, taxes and other situations affecting citrus operations."

One of the last events of the Forties was the freeze of 1949, "which ranks in severity and damage with the historic major freezes of 1913 and 1937," the Exchange reported. An estimated 46,000 carloads of citrus fruit in California and Arizona – just over a third of the region's production – were destroyed by the freeze. "The improved market on oranges and grapefruit was not sufficient to make up for the loss in volume and the costly expenditures for orchard heating," observed the Exchange.

Advertising was drastically reduced. To make matters worse, oranges – for the fifth straight year – were again abnormally small in size. "From the standpoint of quality, flavor and sizes, this is undoubtedly the worst orange crop that was ever marketed from California," the cooperative noted.

DEVELOPMENT OF CANNED FRUIT JUICE PRODUCTS

There was a new factor now present in the citrus marketing situation – the rapid development of canned fruit juice products. By 1949, some 75 percent of the oranges marketed as fresh fruit in the U.S. were ultimately consumed as orange juice. Because canned products were able to be stored from one season to the next, the Exchange began to have to figure in carry-over stocks as well as new crop estimates into its marketing plans.

This meant a change in the way its products operations were viewed. This aspect

The rapid development of canned fruit juice products added a new factor to citrus marketing. Because canned products could be stored season to season, carryover stocks as well as new crop estimates figured in the marketing plans.

could no longer be viewed as a salvage operation for unwanted fresh fruit but as an integral part of the overall marketing operations.

The War had brought changes of many kinds to America, its people and its businesses. Many of the European and Asian markets and people that the Exchange had done business with were now gone. In many cases, rebuilding the cooperative's sales markets from scratch would be necessary.

But in at least one man's mind, change was not only to be expected but perhaps welcomed. "The many trials of this season notwithstanding," wrote Exchange manager Armstrong in 1949, "the citrus industry is filled with opportunities as well as hazards. It will well reward the grower who can produce consistently good crops as to yield, quality and size; and will be a source of worry and concern to the grower who, for any reason, cannot do these things."

The end of World War II would mark the beginning of an era of adjusting to profound national and international events affecting agriculture. From 1945 on, agricultural marketing – for the Exchange and businesses everywhere – was marked by growth, diversification, integration, consolidation, and the modernizing and streamlining of operations.

In California, a new era was dawning, one that would involve – as always – major transformations in the state's land and population. Yet the post-war boom that was turning the agrarian society of Chamblin and Teague into an industrial force was destined to leave a few casualties in its wake.

SUNKIST'S CHAIRMEN AND CHIEF EXECUTIVE OFFICERS

Chairmen of the Board

1893-1894
H.R. Smith - *Los Angeles, California*

1894-1904
A.H. Naftzger - *Riverside, California*

1904-1920
Francis Q. Story - *Alhambra, California*

1920
Peter J. Dreher - *Pomona, California*

1920-1950
Charles C. Teague - *Santa Paula, California*

1950-1965
Harvey A. Lynn - *Riverside, California*

1966-1971
Milton M. Teague - *Santa Paula, California*

1971-1977
John V. Newman - *Ventura, California*

1977-1982
David I. Kline - *Visalia, California*

1982-1985
John V. Newman - *Ventura, California*

1985-1990
Ralph E. Bodine - *San Diego, California*

1990 to present
Thomas N. Dungan - *Exeter, California*

CEO/General Manager/President

1893-1894 W.A. Perry	1896-1897 J.E. Packard	1931-1957 Paul S. Armstrong
1894-1895 E.C. Kimbell	1897-1903 A.H. Naftzger	1957-1965 F.R. Wilcox
1895 A.W. Frost	1903-1904 No general manager (agency days)	1965-1971 Don M. Anderson
1895-1896 A.H. Cargill	1904-1912 B.A. Woodford	1971-1978 Roy Utke
1896 A.W. Frost	1912-1922 G. Harold Powell	1978 to present: Russell L. Hanlin
	1922-1931 Earl G. Dezell	

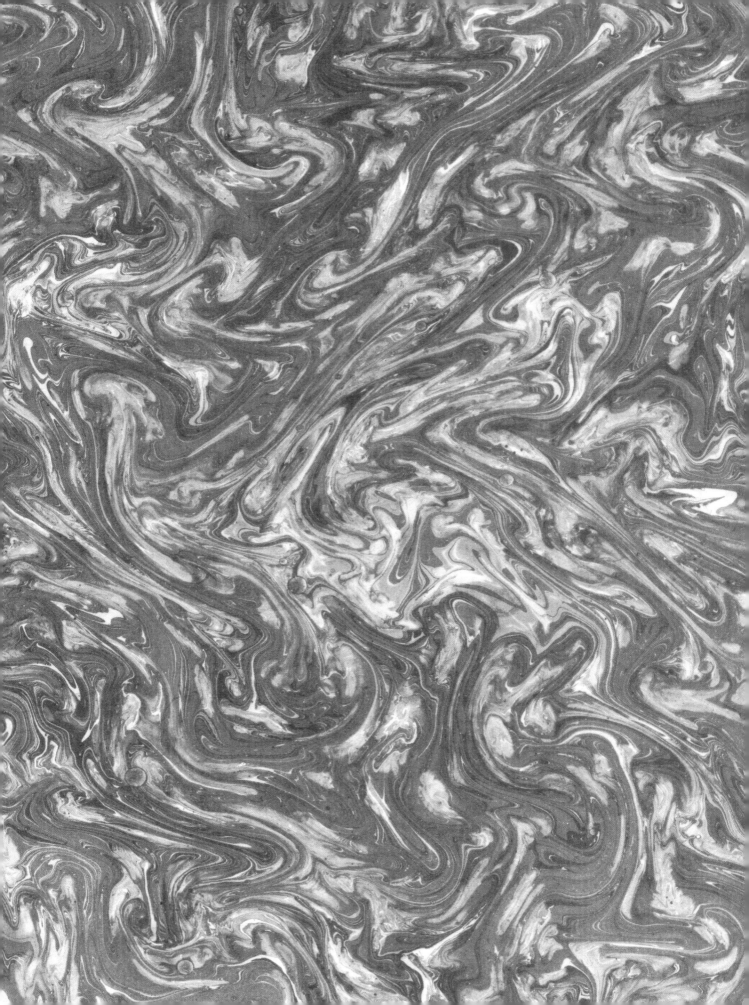

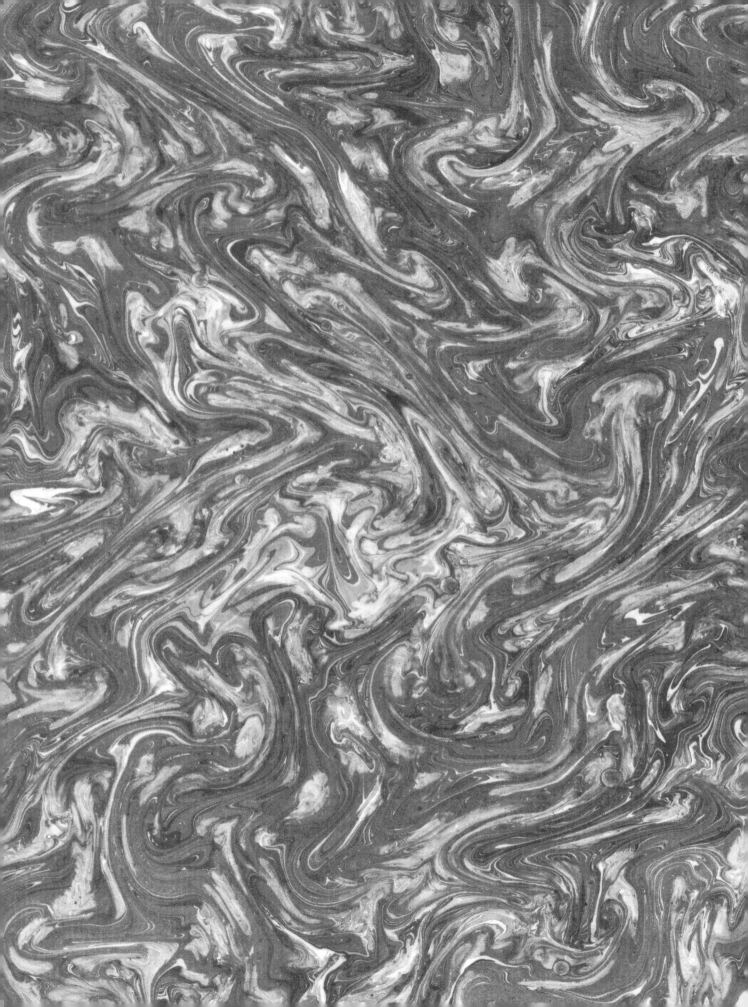

CHAPTER VII – The 1950s

THE OLD MAKES WAY FOR THE NEW

The Fifties would bring unparalleled change, major transitions and the start of a modern era to the Exchange and its grower-members as the world recovered from World War II. Exchange manager Paul S. Armstrong clearly understood what the cooperative and the citrus industry were going through when, in 1953, he said, "Some of these [changes] have been directly beneficial; others have made necessary major changes in methods of operation; while still others have handicapped the industry. We believe however, that on the whole, the changes we have seen will prove to be beneficial in the long run although at times it is difficult to see the benefits immediately."

The decade opened with an event that seemed to symbolize at once the end of an era and the evolution of both the industry and the Exchange.

On March 20, 1950, C.C. Teague, who had been president of the Exchange since 1920, died. He was 76. "Many men have served the organization well over the years, but none with more faithful diligence and distinction than our beloved and respected President, Mr. Charles C. Teague," the Exchange said.

H.A. LYNN BECOMES EXCHANGE PRESIDENT

Teague would be replaced by Riverside's Harvey A. Lynn. Lynn had been in the citrus industry for decades, becoming manager of the Arlington Heights Fruit Exchange in 1914. Later, he had managed the merged Riverside-Arlington Heights Fruit Exchange. In 1921, he had been elected to the board of the Exchange.

In what seemed to be a tradition of sorts, Lynn stepped in just as another problem surfaced. This time, it was a damaging freeze for the second year in succession. Although not as severe as the 1949 freeze, this one brought heavy losses to several districts and some loss to most. Some 30,000 cars of citrus fruit in California and Arizona – or 20 percent of the crop – were destroyed by the cold weather. That which wasn't destroyed saw its quality lowered. Exchange advertising funds were again curtailed.

Despite these adversities, the Exchange, with its astute marketing, brought in over $144 million during the season ended October 31, 1950. Yet production and operating costs – perhaps spurred in part by the outbreak of the conflict in Korea – were increasing in all aspects of the business, from citrus grove to freight line to retail counter. For growers, the net return per acre was often inadequate. Citrus prices did not keep pace with inflation because of the rapid increase in supply, especially in Florida.

The Exchange worked hard to keep its marketing costs low. The cooperative's costs in 1953 amounted to 10.9 cents per box; district exchange costs averaged 1.9 cents per box. The advertising assessment, which had always been separate, was eight cents per box on oranges, three cents on grapefruit, and 14 cents on lemons. During the 1952-53 season, California orange prices averaged $3.34 per box, while lemons brought $6.35.

Harvey Lynn of Riverside served as Exchange president from 1950-65.

SOUTHERN CALIFORNIA CITRUS GROVES DISAPPEAR

Through the Fifties, several major advances would be made by the Exchange in response to the significant and fundamental changes that were occurring across America. A population explosion called "the Baby Boom," the rise of the modern supermarket, an increasing standard of living, and a growing demand for food and other products were re-shaping the nation. In fact, Armstrong would say, "In the years since the end of World War II and particularly since 1950, we have seen perhaps more changes than in the previous quarter of a century."

Of course, in California, these changes involved land and people. Since the end of World War II, there had been a tremendous influx of people moving into California, triggering explosive housing and industrial developments in Southern California. The state's population jumped from 6.9 million people in 1940 to almost 10.6 million by 1950.

First in Los Angeles County and later in Orange County, citrus groves were bulldozed out to make room for new houses, factories, schools and freeways. For those growers still engaged in production, the impact was profound.

"Confronted with constantly mounting costs of labor and material, too often coupled with declining yields," wrote Sunkist general manager Armstrong in 1952, "a good many of the 20,000 growers engaged in this industry are not receiving an adequate return, after all the 'deducts,' to properly maintain their groves and a considerable number of these have not been making expenses for several years past."

Suffering from low prices, many growers in communities near Los Angeles, where property values and taxes were high, decided to sell their citrus farms. By 1950, nearly 20 percent of the planted acreage of what had been – before the War – California's most important agricultural industry, had disappeared. In a 10-year period between 1946 and 1956, citrus land in California and Arizona dropped sharply from 350,000 acres to just 250,000.

AN OLD BRAND BECOMES A NEW NAME

To remain competitive in this environment, citrus marketing was changing. In an aggressive move in 1952, the Exchange re-named itself after one of its most valuable assets. The California Fruit Growers Exchange would forever afterward be known as "Sunkist Growers." As far back as 1917, the "Sunkist" name had been better known to the retail trade and consumers than the rather long "California Fruit Growers Exchange." In fact, *The Sunkist Courier* had noted in 1917, "Eastern representatives report that if on entering a store you introduce yourself as being with the 'Sunkist people,' you are recognized at once and your welcome is assured."

"This change has met with favorable reaction from most everyone," Armstrong reported in 1952. "It brings to our corporate name the best known trademark in the entire field of fresh fruit and vegetables and one of the leading trademarks in America."

In another forward-looking move, Sunkist hired its first electromechanical engineer, Maury Johnson, in 1953 to develop new ways to work on fresh fruit handling. One of Johnson's first assignments was to work with packinghouses that were converting from wooden boxes to new corrugated cartons. But there was much more work at hand. Most of the packinghouses had not been renovated since the 1920s; the great Depression and World War that had followed had hampered their progress. Historically, research and development in Sunkist had been devoted almost exclusively to fruit science. Now, with the arrival of Johnson and the need for packinghouse improvement, a new era of packinghouse automation would begin.

CARTONS BECOME THE STANDARD

By 1954, the standard two-compartment wood box, the industry's packing container for more than 50 years, had been converted to the "fibreboard" carton of one-half box capacity. This change had come about for two reasons. One motivation had been the industry's search to reduce labor costs by simplifying and mechanizing the packinghouse operations as much as possible. The second reason, Sunkist reported, was "the almost universal practice of self-service in retail stores leading to a desire by retailers. . . to have their supplies available in lighter packages."

The Fruit Growers Supply Company began to manufacture "Craveneer," a material using wood veneer available from company mills to insure strength in the cardboard cartons. In fact, as carton usage increased, and the need for sawn shook dropped, the Supply Company began an orderly phasing-out of its mill operations. The mill property at Westwood was "advantageously disposed of," *The Sunkist Courier* would report in 1957. Still, timberland owned by the Supply Company that year totaled nearly 190,000 acres.

In 1954, over 90 percent of Sunkist's lemon shipments and an increasing amount of oranges and grapefruit were shipped in the cartons. And as the old made way for the new, the colorful, distinctive labels which had long adorned wooden shipping boxes would vanish. Now, the name of the packinghouse and its own brand as well as the Sunkist brand would be preprinted on the carton.

Beginning with the 1955-56 year, all orders, quotations, accounting, and other records switched from a box basis to a carton basis. "Thus, a tradition of the industry almost from the very inception changes as many others have changed over the years," Armstrong noted. "It may take a little time for an older operating man to become accustomed to the fact that a carton of 100's is really a 200 size orange."

One of the casualties of the cardboard cartons was the paper wrapper, which for

A major change in the 1950s was the transition of wooden shipping crate to cardboard box.   Top inset: The 1950s saw the standard two-compartment wooden box phased out of packinghouse operations.   Left inset: Maury Johnson – Virtually all machinery found in a 1990s packinghouse was invented or modernized under the supervision of Sunkist engineer Maury Johnson, whose work spanned nearly 40 years, beginning in the 1950s.

114

PACKINGHOUSES: VITAL TO THE INDUSTRY

Packinghouses – or local associations – are intrinsic to Sunkist, serving as one level in the cooperative's three-tiered membership structure and providing the vital role of preparing growers' fruit for market.

The packinghouse role has changed considerably in the last 100 years. In the early days, there were hundreds of packinghouses throughout California. Some would be owned by two or three people, maybe a family. Such a packinghouse might stay open for only a month, and pack only valencia oranges. Back then, of course, fruit packing was done by hand, each piece of citrus individually wrapped in a piece of tissue paper and placed in a wooden crate. And, too, packinghouses handled the citrus only for the fresh fruit market. Many of these associations had their own brand names in addition to "Sunkist" to identify to the trade the quality of their own local fruit.

The modernization of the industry changed the citrus packinghouse. In the 1920s, there were over 200 packing associations in the Sunkist network. By 1992, there were only 66 packinghouses in the system. Packinghouses had become larger, sophisticated facilities.

Technology brought automation, labor-saving equipment and high technology to the packinghouses. By the 1990s, equipment for sizing, grading, color sorting, and pattern packing was computerized – much of the machinery found in a modern packing plant had been invented and manufactured by

Sunkist, under the direction of Maury Johnson. He played a significant role in designing and developing the lemon volumetric sizer, the lemon volume filling machine, the "soft touch" pack machine, bulk bin dumpers, and the enzyme peeling project. He was also a major contributor in the development of the place packer, the electromechanical grader, the sectionizer, and the electro-optical sizer.

Today, quality is paramount at a Sunkist packinghouse. The packinghouse manager usually decides when fruit will be harvested and supervises the picking and hauling. At the packinghouse, the fruit is washed and dried, graded and sized, packed and cooled, and the cartons are loaded for shipment. While the cartons will advertise the Sunkist name, the association's local brand name will also be imprinted on the container.

The biggest packinghouses, like the Saticoy Lemon Association, may handle as many as 7 million cartons a year. They may represent 250 grower-member entities from 12,000 acres. At the peak of the January through June season, these large houses may employ as many as 1,200 fruit pickers out in the groves, and 500 full-time packers.

As part of Sunkist's federated structure, packinghouses are either grower-owned associations which are members of Sunkist, or they are packing facilities which are licensed to pack the fruit of Sunkist growers. In either case, they cannot pack fruit for anyone but Sunkist growers. This keeps both the cooperative's quality control and its funding assessments in order.

years had enveloped each piece of fruit to identify its Sunkist origins. Without the paper wrapper, there suddenly was no trademark on lemons.

Spurred by Russ Eller, the head of Sunkist advertising, the cooperative sought a lemon trademarking machine that would allow lemon shippers to place the famous Sunkist trademark on the yellow fruit. Trademarking onto the round oranges had been in place for years, but branding the elongated lemons was more difficult. The challenge was to do it quickly, at low cost and without injuring the fruit. The machine was finally developed, culminating several years of intensive work on the part of Sunkist personnel. The successful trademarking of lemons now assured consumers they were buying Sunkist's top quality fruit.

There were other changes too. A new teletype system linking Exchange sales offices was completed, providing better and more rapid communication with its sales offices at lower cost.

ENTERING THE FROZEN CONCENTRATE ARENA

The Exchange would take another significant step in 1951 when it began branding its famous "Sunkist" trademark on frozen concentrates and other canned citrus juices. Sunkist had been watching the market skyrocket for these products and it had felt the competition from Texas and Florida citrus producers.

The cooperative had long recognized the power of its Sunkist brand as a way to remain a strong marketing entity. In the fall of 1950, it acquired all U.S. and foreign rights to the Sunkist trademark owned by the California Packing Corporation. Cal-Pak had been using the Sunkist brand name for over 40 years on a full line (exclusive of citrus products) of canned vegetables and other grocery items. Once the Exchange acquired exclusive rights to the name, close vigilance in protecting the Sunkist trademark became necessary.

Reflecting the growing importance of citrus by-products, especially frozen concentrates, the Exchange Lemon Products Company acquired the Damerel-Allison plant at Covina in 1950. Its purchase price was just over $1 million. The facility would sharply increase the capacity of the Exchange Lemon Products Company in the production of frozen lemonade concentrate.

In addition, construction was started on a new juice products manufacturing plant for the consolidation and expansion of the company's canning and freezing facilities at Corona. In 1952, the new addition was completed at the cost of $2 million. The Exchange Lemon Products Company was now the oldest and largest lemon processor in the world.

And, for the twentieth consecutive year, both the orange and lemon products companies showed an increase in gross dollar sales, with the 1949-50 season bringing in $22.5 million. In 1951, The Exchange Orange Products Company set a record in tonnage of

Sunkist began branding its name onto its frozen canned concentrates in late 1950 – a significant step towards utilizing the power of its brand.   Inset: Demand for orange juice skyrocketed in the 1950s. By 1955, Sunkist operated five plants in California and Arizona for the production of citrus products like juice.

valencia and miscellaneous oranges handled during a season, reaching almost 300,000 tons. The Exchange found huge competition in this arena, as production of concentrated juices surged in Florida and Texas.

Yet the Exchange kept pace with the competition. By 1955, its products department – the sales arm for both the orange and lemon products companies – had helped the sales of citrus products double in the previous five years. Products were produced at five plants located at Ontario, Corona, Covina, Lindsay, and Tempe, Arizona. New office facilities for Sunkist's products department were built in Ontario in 1955.

OLD INDUSTRY TRADITIONS DISAPPEAR

In addition to the wooden boxes and paper wrappers, among the casualties of the Fifties were long-time district exchanges which were terminating operations. In 1953, the Semi-Tropic Fruit Exchange, one of the seven original districts to form the old Southern California Fruit Exchange in 1893, ceased operations. That year, too, the San Dimas Fruit Exchange also closed down.

Growers, too, were making changes. Coming home from World War II, many of them had been eager to build their careers and farms. Although many knew they would have to leave increasingly urban Southern California, they wanted to remain in the industry which had represented a way of life to them. After selling their ranches in Southern California at profitable prices, many citrus growers began looking for new lands to farm.

They would find them in the nearby San Joaquin Valley and Arizona. Irrigation projects were opening up new land for farming in California's great Central Valley, and in the arid desert country of Arizona and southeastern California. Another incentive to farmers was availability of land in Arizona for "homesteading" under provisions of federal law. The West's citrus industry, far from going out of business, would get a new breath of life.

A CHERISHED ENTERPRISE

Despite the shift in area of production from Southern to Central California, citrus remained the state's major food crop. In the U.S., the consumption of citrus fruits was equal to that of all other fruits combined.

In the mid-1950s, Americans were spending 9.13 cents on fresh fruits and vegetables for every dollar they paid out for food, according to a speech by Armstrong, then Sunkist's general manager. "Dealing as we are, with a natural fruit, which is not novel or possessed of improved new features, we maintain an unremitting quest for new facts of health and consumer usefulness," Armstrong said, "and invest substantial sums each year in scientific research to this end. It is surprising how many new angles turn up every year or so."

Whether it was fresh, canned, dried, or frozen, citrus fruit in some form comprised 50

The coolingest cooler of all - Sunkist Lemonade

THERE YOU ARE. Stretched out in the shade. A tall, frosty glass of fresh Sunkist lemonade in your hand. You sip it, enjoy its tangy, fresh fragrance. You take a long, cold swallow. And suddenly...*coolness*. Deep. All through you.

There's your proof. Lemonade refreshes more thoroughly than any other summer drink. The reason is simple. Lemon juice replaces vitamin C and other energy-giving vitamins that warm weather takes away.

For true lemon flavor and long-lasting refreshment, drink Sunkist lemonade. Lots of it. Sunkist Lemons are the pick of the crop!

TRY FRESH LEMON WITH ICED TEA! Lemon brings out the flavor and delicate aroma of the tea, adds a subtle, delicious tang, makes it even more cooling and refreshing. Iced tea... wedges of lemon... wonderful for sparking up summer meals! Remember lemons—today.

NOW—Sunkist FROZEN LEMONADE! When you're extra busy, here's delicious lemonade we make *for* you. A fine, new Sunkist product now coming on the market. Just add water and ice. *Easy. Healthful. Refreshing!* Look for it! **FRESH OR FROZEN, IT'S BEST WHEN IT'S Sunkist!**

Sunkist Lemons FROM CALIFORNIA

Throughout the 1950s Sunkist continued to promote its citrus featuring the superior value of fresh fruit and freshly squeezed juice as well as quick-frozen lemonade and emphasizing nutritional and health benefits.

percent of the total consumption of all fruits combined. Sunkist could well claim a role in that development.

"Growers affiliated with Sunkist can well take pride in the fact that their organization was chiefly instrumental in developing and maintaining demand over a long period of years," Armstrong remarked in 1955.

Sunkist could also take pride in the strength of its membership base. Throughout the changes in area of production, Sunkist membership had remained remarkably strong. In 1955, Sunkist handled over 70 percent of the California-Arizona citrus crop. The cooperative counted 12,500 members – all part-owners of the business. The average grower owned about 16 acres.

"Every grower is anxious to make a success of his own personal business," Armstrong wrote, "but even the largest does not have the production volume or the resources to conduct marketing operations for himself on an effective scale. As an individual, he cannot afford the advertising, the research, the market development so necessary to successful selling today."

Sunkist was now spending some $3 million per year on advertising, under the direction of Russ Eller who had held that position since 1939. Since that first Iowa campaign back in 1908, the cooperative had invested an aggregate of $72 million on advertising, according to Armstrong. In fact, Sunkist remained the only citrus marketing organization in California or Arizona with a national advertising program.

Just as important to Sunkist was its research. The cooperative now had a packaging program using polyethylene bags for five-pound sacks of oranges for consumer purchase. And in 1953, the health importance of citrus bioflavonoids and protopectins – discovered over many years of research – became a key theme in Sunkist's "Oranges for Health" advertising.

"What continues to amaze me, after working all of my business life in Sunkist, is the fact that the persons who conceived this complicated business structure in 1893 were able to construct it so that the incentives for individual excellence of production were meticulously established and preserved," Armstrong noted in 1955, "so the organization has weathered all sorts of economic conditions over the years and has maintained a voluntary membership, subject to annual withdrawal, of three-fourths of all the growers producing citrus fruits in California and Arizona. This cooperative marketing organization is a prime example of free enterprise which we cherish in America."

ADDITIONAL DEVELOPMENTS

The Exchange Orange Products Company and Exchange Lemon Products Company grew steadily. By 1954, they were bringing in over $32 million a year from the sale of juice and other products. By the late Fifties, more than 400 items were being marketed by Sunkist's products department. Every development helped add revenue to growers' pockets as the products companies continued to find ways to utilize every part of the fruit, from peel to pulp.

In 1957, Sunkist's field laboratory in Ontario was separated from the field department and made a part of the research department. By 1958, one of the laboratory's designs – a lemon sizer – was being installed by almost all lemon packinghouses. The equipment resulted in a vast improvement in lemon sizing at a lower cost to the associations.

Sunkist also initiated an export licensing program to sell citrus products and generate additional revenues from the use of the Sunkist trademark. By the early Fifties, Sunkist had a licensing program permitting the use of its trademark on a quality, ready-to-drink lemonade through dairies.

Celebrating its fiftieth anniversary in 1957, the Fruit Growers Supply Company could report that its volume of business during that half century had totaled well over $630 million, and cash returned to members in the form of dividends and refunds had reached over $36 million. (There would be a personal tragedy for the Supply Company when in April 1958, its general manager, H.A. Thomas, was killed in a plane crash.)

ARMSTRONG RETIRES

In another major transformation, general manager Armstrong retired from Sunkist on January 1, 1957 after nearly 41 years of service to the cooperative.

"From the time he joined the Sunkist staff as a dealer service man in 1916, he has been interested in only one project: the continued strength and success of the Sunkist organization," wrote board president Harvey A. Lynn. "As general manager he successfully led Sunkist through a great depression and a world-encompassing war into a period which has seen more fundamental changes in citrus marketing than any previous time in the history of the industry. . . . In this he was eminently successful. . . . Sunkist people everywhere will miss Paul Armstrong."

In his last annual report in 1956, Armstrong wrote, "On many occasions, I have expressed my unfaltering faith in our industry and its future. There will always be changes in it, and changes are usually accompanied by progress."

And displaying the prophetic abilities he had always shown, Armstrong closed his 40-year Sunkist career with a quote from the Roman philosopher Cato, echoing his remarks from two thousand years earlier, "The wise man does no wrong in changing his habits with the times."

Armstrong's successor would be Francis R. Wilcox, Sunkist's long-time assistant general manager. The Sunkist board also named Don M. Anderson as assistant general manager and secretary, and M.D. Street as treasurer.

Wilcox, who had joined Sunkist in 1939 as director of marketing research, took the

Francis R. Wilcox, Sunkist's general manager from 1957-65.

helm just as the cooperative was celebrating the fiftieth anniversary of its advertising program. Sunkist was the oldest and the most consistent advertiser in the perishable foods field and one of the oldest in the entire food marketing picture. "There is no question but that this long record of consistent, well planned advertising has meant millions of dollars affiliated with Sunkist – returns far in excess of the amount invested in advertising," Wilcox observed.

The cooperative continued to promote its oranges and lemons in America's best-read publications, like *The Saturday Evening Post, Life* and *Look* magazines. The ads emphasized the superior value of fresh oranges and freshly squeezed juice, as well as lemons and quick-frozen lemonade, both calling attention to nutritional and health characteristics.

And Sunkist stood out in other areas. By 1958, no other marketing organization in the world had a more complex, high-speed communications system than Sunkist. Instant teletype messages could be transmitted, thus assuring quick action on all sales transactions.

To help maintain Sunkist's reputation for quality – one of its strongest business assets – some 40 Sunkist field inspectors continually checked the fruit from grove to packinghouse. Sunkist representatives even checked the icing of freight cars – all as a quality safeguard of the fruit from tree to market.

Its dealer service men – or "merchandisers" as they were now called – played a vital part in linking Sunkist advertising to the fruit in the store through effective merchandising and point-of-purchase displays.

PRODUCTS COMPANIES MERGE

One of the single biggest events of the 1950s occurred on November 1, 1958, when – in a reorganization of Sunkist's corporate structure – Exchange Lemon Products Company and The Exchange Orange Products Company merged with Sunkist Growers, Inc.

The objective of the merger, Wilcox reported, "was to permit the most efficient use of the products and marketing facilities owned by the citrus growers affiliated with Sunkist." What had been the Exchange Lemon Products Company would now be the lemon products division of Sunkist Growers and would be headed by D.F. McMillen. J.A. Finley would direct the orange products division. Overseeing sales of products for both departments would be D.R. Thompson.

Sunkist's board and management had been concerned that the three closely-linked entities – fresh fruit, lemon products and orange products – might be considered legally an improper combination or restraint of trade. By combining them, they would form an organization under one management.

The combination of the three brought an expansion in the size of Sunkist's board of directors from 17 to 31 members. Originally organized on the basis of one director for each district exchange with no regard for volume handled, Sunkist that year decided to in-

By the mid-1950s, Americans' consumption of citrus fruit was equal to that of all other fruits combined – an achievement for which Sunkist's promotion could take credit.

crease board representation based on total volume of fruit handled by the exchange. While basic policies would still be determined by the board, a products executive committee of 15 members was formed to keep a focus on the complex products operations.

Under the new structure, packinghouse associations and district exchanges became direct members of the federated Sunkist organization.

Yet, the action would result in problems down the road for Sunkist. Alleging monopolization and arguing that the newly reorganized Sunkist no longer qualified as a cooperative under the 1922 Capper-Volstead Act, a competitor in the processed products industry filed a private anti-trust suit in 1958 against the organization. The case would remain in the federal courts for ten years before the U.S. Supreme Court handed down its decision on the suit.

Sunkist was still adjusting to profound change as the Fifties came to an end. There was a depressed – and oversupplied – lemon market. Tristeza, a strange new "quick decline" virus, was moving through orchards all over Southern California. There was the growing cost of raising citrus fruit in an increasingly urban state. Between 1950 and 1960, the Golden State had picked up 5 million people to reach a population of 15.7 million inhabitants.

Even more importantly, the focus of Sunkist's sales efforts was about to shift dramatically as many of the ravaged nations of the world began to emerge from the ashes of World War II.

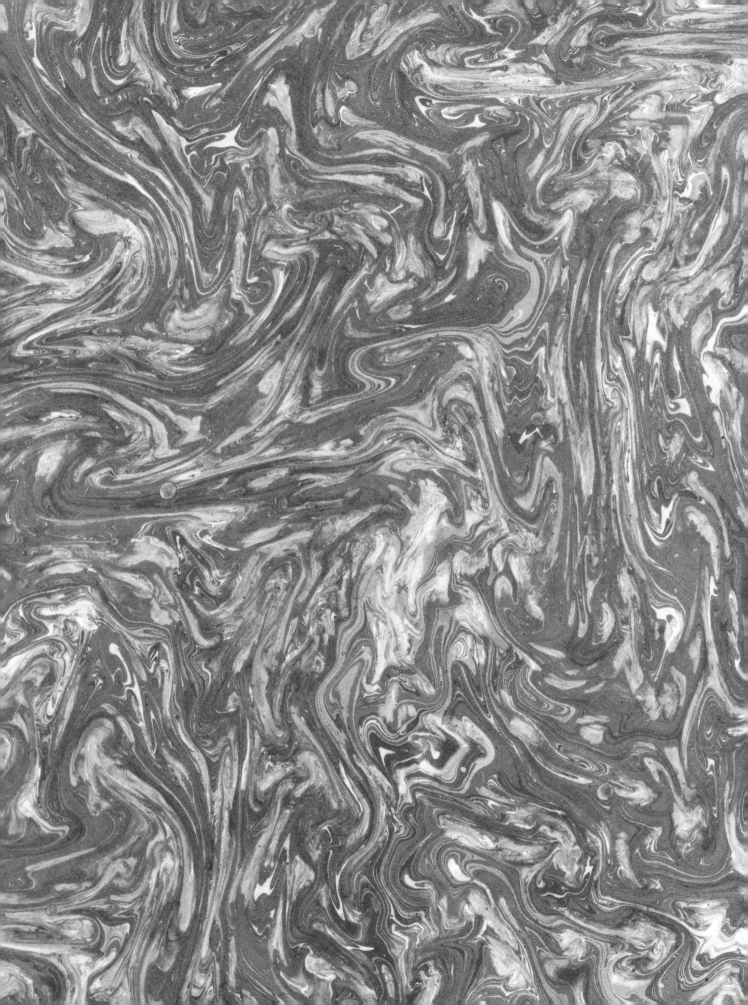

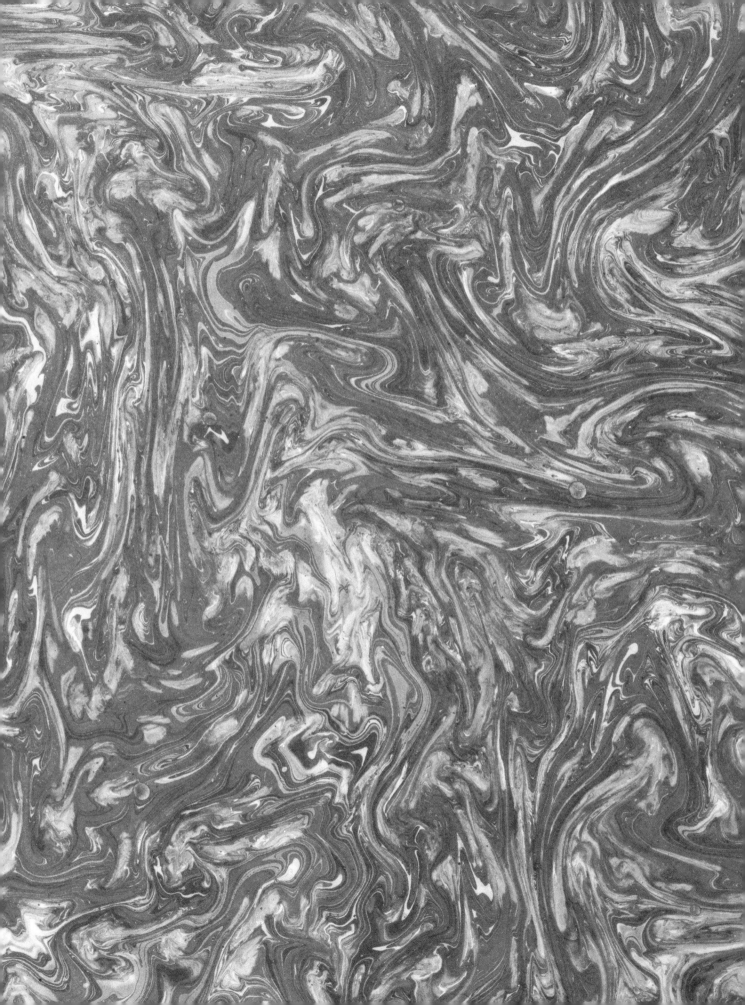

CHAPTER VIII – The 1960s

MAINTAINING LEADERSHIP

Sunkist's export business boomed as Europe and Asia recovered from World War II. Throughout the 1960s, increasingly larger shipments of fresh citrus left the docks at the Port of Long Beach.

The great sweep of change which had begun after World War II continued to dominate American society and businesses as the 1960s began. Sunkist was far from believing that the rapid pace of change was about to slow down. "While the acreage shifts which have taken place since the close of the World War II have been more far-reaching than any of us had anticipated, the continuation of these changes throughout the Sixties may be of equal magnitude," Sunkist's general manager F.R. Wilcox cautioned in 1960.

Perhaps nothing would change the culture of America's food marketers as profoundly as the advent of the modern supermarket and the growth of export markets which began in the Sixties. These two developments would shape the citrus industry – and Sunkist - for the next 20 years.

DEVELOPING WORLDWIDE MARKETS

As the war-battered countries of Europe and Asia restored their industries and developed their economies – astounding America with their success – they could begin buying discretionary food products such as citrus. The European markets would open first, helped by massive aid programs designed to help speed recovery there. Although it had to contend with competition from foreign citrus producers, Sunkist began broadening its overseas scope to capitalize on the opportunities abroad.

Under the direction of its export manager Robert Autenreith, Sr., the organization undertook daring operations to ship its fruit to Europe on consignment. It was a risk to send fruit without a sale having already been made but one the cooperative's board of directors chose to take because there were so few other outlets for the tremendous citrus surplus of the time. The consignment sales to Europe would prove successful.

During the 1963-64 season, Sunkist shipped almost 7.9 million cartons abroad, most to Europe. The cooperative was especially pleased when, in May 1964, slow-opening Japan removed license restrictions on lemon imports. "We are planning an intensive sales and advertising campaign for the 1964-65 season to maintain and further develop the potential of this preferred market," Wilcox said.

Highly successful Sunkist soft drink operations were flourishing throughout Europe as well as in Hong Kong and Japan. These international licensees were spending their own monies to advertise and merchandise both the unique Tetra-Pak container and bottled soft drinks bearing the Sunkist name.

By the 1966-67 season, exports achieved an all-time high of 12.4 million cartons, reaching markets from Tokyo to Hamburg, and Paris to Papeete. Europe would remain the major overseas market of the Sixties, absorbing nearly 10 million cartons of Sunkist fruit at its peak.

Japan alone accounted for well over a million cartons annually by the mid-1960s. With newly appointed agents in Hong Kong, Singapore, the Philippines, Okinawa, and Tahiti, Sunkist now had direct representation in all of its export markets. Nearly 20 percent of all Sunkist fresh fruit shipments were being distributed overseas. In 1967, under Autenreith, Sunkist arranged its first special fully refrigerated ship for the Far East. The vessel carried a total cargo of 105,000 cartons of fruit to Japan and Hong Kong. And, of course, because the quality of Sunkist fruit was considered the best, it received premium prices.

SUPERMARKETS EMERGE, DEALER SERVICE AND AUCTIONS DISAPPEAR

The opening of these markets couldn't have come at a better time for Sunkist. By the Sixties, the post-War "Baby Boom" had slowed and population in the U.S. had stabilized. The heavy citrus plantings of the 1950s were resulting in over-production and surplus.

With the advent of the supermarket, the food industry had grown larger, more sophisticated and more complex. Retail chains operated much differently than the small grocery stores, and this was changing the network of selling and shipping. In the process, two long-time citrus industry traditions were being phased out.

For years, Sunkist's dealer service division had played an important role in merchandising the cooperative's fruit in grocery stores around the nation. Its dealer service representatives had supplied the stores with point-of-sale material and helped build displays. But modern supermarkets, with their streamlined and integrated approach, wanted total control of their own environment. They directed their own advertising, their own ordering, their own inventory control. Demand for Sunkist's dealer service men began dropping in the Sixties; by the 1970s, they were gone.

As the supermarkets built in importance, they also helped end another piece of industry history. Supermarkets bought their supplies in enormous quantities and in advance. In many ways, this was beneficial for Sunkist, for the chains often purchased their produce from source suppliers. But massive advance buying could not be satisfied by the produce auctions in the East, where daily bids and orders of fruits and vegetables had gone on for years. Accustomed to smaller orders and fluctuating bids from individually owned grocery stores, the auctions could not compete. By the end of the 1970s, they too would be gone.

When the auctions disappeared, they took with them a safety valve Sunkist had long used. In the past, whenever Sunkist had fewer buyers or outlets for the fruit that packinghouses needed to pack, the cooperative allowed packinghouses to unilaterally send fruit to the auctions. As the fruit rolled East, Sunkist could attempt to sell it en route. But if it made it to the auction unsold, there was always the option of selling the fruit there.

When the auctions dried up, the pressure to sell – not only every box and carton but at a "good" price – fell increasingly on Sunkist's sales department. This would become one of the major changes for the cooperative, as it adjusted to the scramble of taking full responsibility for selling every box of a perishable commodity without a safety valve. Every sale would become a direct sale with a firm price, and citrus-selling a much more high pressure business.

STAYING ON TOP

Sunkist fully intended to maintain its leadership of the citrus industry. Since its founding in 1893, Sunkist sales of members' fruit had exceeded $6.8 billion. U.S. per capita consumption of citrus fruit in all forms had risen from 18 pounds in 1910 to 86 pounds in 1960. Sunkist sales for the 1959-60 season reached $223 million. Despite the advances its orange and lemon products divisions had made, Sunkist's primary revenue earner remained fresh fruit. The cooperative continued to handle over 70 percent of the Far West citrus crop. By the early Sixties, Sunkist had also begun to market tangerines.

Yet even with this track record, Sunkist could not rest. "No greater error could be committed by a marketing organization than to permit itself to become mired in the glories of its past," general manager Wilcox cautioned.

"We are painfully aware that in most instances per capita consumption, not only of citrus but of most fresh fruits and vegetables is declining," Wilcox reported in 1961. "I believe, without qualification, this is Sunkist's greatest marketing challenge."

To keep its dominant place, Sunkist recognized that meeting its members' needs and concerns was essential. In that respect, Sunkist would have to remain as efficient and cost-effective as possible. During the first year of the decade, Sunkist's board of directors had approved an extensive revision of its organizational structure for management.

This was actually the result of the 1958 merger of Sunkist Growers, Exchange Lemon Products Company and The Exchange Orange Products Company. Six major activities now reported directly to the general manager: marketing, administration, treasurer, secretary and legal counsel, orange products division, and lemon products division. With these six divisional managers reporting directly to the general manager, the office of assistant general manager was discontinued and the director of marketing named senior authority immediately below the general manager. The new director of marketing would be D.M. Anderson.

RESEARCH INTENSIFIED

Research would also remain a priority with Sunkist. A highlight in 1962 was the Sunkist development of Perma-Stabil® citrus flavors. This event was the result of intensified essential oil research which extended the industrial use of peel products in both the domestic and export markets. The inventor of the process was Horton E. Swisher, chief chemist of the Sunkist research laboratory in Ontario. Everyone involved in the Sunkist association took pride that year when the process won the coveted Food Technology Industrial Achievement Award for 1962 – the highest award in the food industry.

Looking for new products to help increase the demand for lemons, Sunkist intro-

The development of the Perma-Stabil® process, invented in 1962 by Sunkist's chief chemist Horton E. Swisher, earned the cooperative the food industry's highest honor – the Food Technology Industrial Achievement Award. Perma-Stabil helped lock in citrus flavor in a number of products.

duced two new products on the national market in 1960. One was the Sunkist fruit-lemon punch; the other, frozen fruit bars.

An amazing number of Sunkist Juicit Extractors – born long before as a result of Sunkist development – continued to be offered for home and restaurant use. Thousands were sold, each extractor meaning additional demand for fresh citrus.

New product development was so strong that by the late Sixties, well over 100 U.S. patents had been issued to Sunkist as a result of discoveries by its research people.

By 1965, many packinghouses were operating with a Sunkist-designed "place-pack" machine, which quickly, gently and systematically packed fruit through the use of rubber vacuum cups. Up to 2,000 40-pound cartons could be packed in an eight-hour shift, compared to the hand packer's average of 330 cartons a day.

Sunkist also intensified its research efforts towards mechanically-assisted harvesting systems. A single-clip lemon clipper had also been developed by Sunkist's field research and engineering department. The device was designed to clip the lemon at the button on the first clip, speeding picking operations from the former two-clip procedure.

ADVERTISING ENTERS TELEVISION

To maintain leadership, advertising would also remain vital. Seeing the effect that television could have on American society – evidenced by its role in helping John F. Kennedy defeat Richard M. Nixon for U.S. President in 1960 – Sunkist began using televised commercials in the 1960s.

In a radical departure from campaigns of previous years, Sunkist in the 1962-63 season confined its fresh lemon promotion to 60-second black-and-white commercials which aired on seven ABC-TV daytime network shows. With this avenue, Sunkist's lemon commercials reached into 30 million homes about eight times that season.

By the next year, Sunkist's television advertising had broadened to include oranges. Commercials ran on hundreds of stations in the U.S. and Canada. The first color commercial ever to be telecast on behalf of any fresh fruit aired in the summer of 1965, when Sunkist featured its lemons on both NBC and CBS stations around the country.

Newspaper coupons were used in Sunkist's advertising in the 1965-66 season for the first time on a major scale. Returns were excellent for both sales results and redemptions.

GROWERS FACE CHALLENGES

Out in the groves, growers continued to face challenges. In addition to loss of acreage to urban development in Southern California, the "quick decline" virus was contributing to a loss of trees in Los Angeles, Orange, San Bernardino, Riverside, and Ventura Counties. By 1962, it had even spread to San Diego County. This "virus attacked sour root orange stock and when it hit a grove, the trees would die within a very short time, even in days," it was reported in the *Pomona Centennial History*. Over the decade, the virus would be battled with a replanting program that replaced infected trees.

There were new faces in citrus-growing circles. So dramatic was the shift that by 1965, 60 percent of the growers affiliated with Sunkist had not even been in the citrus business 15 years earlier. And the average acreage of the individual grower had increased substantially since 1950, since most of the new plantings were so much larger than the old groves, which had usually totaled 10 to 20 acres in size.

By the middle of the 1960s, Sunkist's total numbers of growers had diminished. It now had 103 active associations representing some 8,000 growers, this down sharply from the 14,000 members who once owned the cooperative. Yet Sunkist continued to handle over 75 percent of the Far West's citrus volume. The citrus production of Sunkist growers now centered in the San Joaquin Valley, Riverside and Ventura Counties, and in the Arizona area extending from Yuma to the Salt River Valley.

And new citrus production – the heavy navel orange plantings in Central California and increased valencia orange plantings in the desert – was about to come to harvest. In 1965, total citrus acreage – bearing and non-bearing – in California and Arizona totaled 295,000 acres. By 1971, it would reach over 355,000.

WILCOX SUCCEEDED BY ANDERSON

The Sixties saw other transformations take place inside Sunkist. In 1964, F.R. Wilcox served his last year as Sunkist general manager, retiring after 25 years with the cooperative. In his final report to the Sunkist board and membership, Wilcox wrote, "Just as vigilance is the price of liberty, diligence is the price of leadership. This diligence must encompass economic . . . technical and marketing research. . . . Policies must be re-examined, not simply for the sake of re-examination but rather to be sure they continue to serve Sunkist's prime purpose."

Wilcox would be succeeded by D.M. Anderson in the office of Sunkist general manager. Anderson had joined Sunkist in 1931 as a merchandiser. His assignments had carried him to the 44 states where Sunkist had sales districts. He had steadily moved up the ranks through the years. Like his predecessor, Anderson was well aware of the challenges facing the industry and Sunkist.

The 1966 year also brought memories of the past when, in January, Milton M. Teague – son of C.C. Teague – was elected president of Sunkist's board of directors, taking the place of Harvey A. Lynn. Lynn would go on to expand his citrus interests in the Coachella Valley. Later that year, Lynn unanimously was named President Emeritus of Sunkist – the first ever – in recognition of his 45 years of service on the board.

Teague held a degree from Stanford University, and, following his father's example, had managed the Limoneira Company in Santa Paula. He had been a member of Sunkist's

Milton M. Teague – son of long-time Exchange president Charles Teague – served as Sunkist's board chairman from 1966-71.

D.M. Anderson, Sunkist's general manager from 1965-71, presided over the move of Sunkist's headquarters from Los Angeles to Sherman Oaks.

The Fruit Growers Supply Company teamed up with the Zellerbach Paper Company in 1961 to build adjoining plants in the City of Industry in Los Angeles County. Together, they produced corrugated cardboard cartons for shipping Sunkist members' fruit.

board of directors since 1950, when he had taken over the vacancy created by his father's death.

The cooperative was primed to hold onto its leadership. And having buckled down to meet the challenges of the Sixties, Sunkist was soon setting new records in sales and shipments.

SUNKIST PROGRESSES

By the latter half of the Sixties, Sunkist was handling almost 80 percent of the Far West citrus volume. Its delivered sales for the 1966-67 season were then the highest in its history at $285 million. The 101 million equivalent cartons it handled of fresh and processed fruit also set a new record that year.

Sales expansion was not only necessary because of the increased production, but there was always the unknown element of size and grade. "An agricultural product is a product of nature," Anderson noted after the 1966-67 season produced fruit sizes of extreme contrasts. "If citrus fruit were produced, precision-like on a machine line, there would be no such problem for every fruit could be precisely what the customer wanted. This is not possible with an agricultural product."

By this time, the Fruit Growers Supply Company was generating $20 million a year in purchases for grower-members. This included handling orders for more than 64 million shipping cartons, and enormous amounts of diphenyl liners for boxes, irrigation pipe, orchard thermometers, picking bags, and conveyer belts. In addition, the Supply Company sold millions of dollars worth of commercial lumber and 70,000 Christmas trees.

In 1961, the Supply Company embarked on a partnership with a well-known paper manufacturer to benefit the members of Sunkist. It began construction on a new carton plant in the City of Industry in Los Angeles County. Next to it, the Crown Zellerbach Company was breaking ground on its own facility. The Crown plant would produce corrugated sheets which would then be conveyed next door to the Supply Company to be made into shipping cartons for Sunkist citrus shippers. In 1964, the adjoining plants would win a Los Angeles Beautiful Community Award for outstanding landscaping and good exterior housekeeping.

75th ANNIVERSARY FILLED WITH FRUSTRATIONS

There remained, as always, the threat of a damaging freeze. California citrus growers were hit with just such a disaster in December 1967, when a major freeze hit Central California with extremely low temperatures of long duration. Fruit damage was extreme. In January 1968, a second freeze hit the same area, nipping the fruit that had escaped severe damage from the earlier frost. Southern California and Arizona escaped the freeze. Central California, now a major citrus producing region, was not so fortunate.

In what was planned to be a year of celebration, as Sunkist Growers prepared to com-

GOVERNOR REAGAN SALUTES SUNKIST'S 75th

"Your success in joining together – motivated by desire to succeed without governmental in-terference and without short-sighted greed – to cooperatively control your industry's output of the valuable citrus commodity stirs me to pass on my hearty congratulations. . . . You will profit and you will grow. . . . Let everyone know about it – keep the state and the nation and the world informed by the fact that by your example, strength builds strength – that profit is not a dirty word."

- California Governor Ronald Reagan, 1968, on the occasion of Sunkist's 75th anniversary memorate its 75th anniversary, the cooperative took immediate steps to drastically reduce all unnecessary activities. Sunkist's scheduled all-out use of color television was trimmed to the bone. Many planned sales promotions were canceled. Travel was restricted and phone and other communications charges reduced.

Sunkist's delivered sales that season dropped $33 million from a year earlier to $252 million. Total volume of all varieties of citrus handled fell 23.5 million to 43.5 million cartons.

And, then, as if the devastating freeze had not been enough, Sunkist was hit with another blow.

LEGAL MATTERS FORCE SUNKIST TO REORGANIZE

Since 1958, Sunkist had been a defendant in a suit in which damages of approximately $6.6 million were being sought for alleged violation of federal antitrust acts. This action had been dismissed by the U.S. District Court in December 1964 and had been submitted by the plaintiff – Case-Swayne Co., Inc. – to appellate review.

The judgment in favor of Sunkist by the U.S. District Court was reversed by the U.S. District Court of Appeals in November 1966, resulting in the action being remanded to the District Court for retrial and the plaintiff being permitted to file a supplemental complaint.

In October 1967 the United States Supreme Court heard arguments regarding the applicability of the Capper-Volstead Act to Sunkist Growers, Inc., in a response to the suit filed by Case-Swayne Co., Inc.

In December 1967, the blow came. The U.S. Supreme Court ruled that Sunkist Growers, Inc. did not qualify as a bona fide agricultural cooperative under the provisions of the Capper-Volstead Act. The reason, the Court said, was because Sunkist had members who were not producers or associations of producers.

In response to the Supreme Court decision, Sunkist was substantially reorganized in 1968 to ensure compliance with the Capper-Volstead Act. The organization would remain a federated cooperative, only now it would have three classes of members: growers, local co-op packinghouses and regional "district exchanges." Each grower would hold individual membership in Sunkist, and also be affiliated with a local packinghouse. Not all packinghouses would be grower-owned. Some would be considered non-member commercial packers, licensed by Sunkist and a district exchange to pack fruit on a fee basis for Sunkist growers.

By 1968, Sunkist was composed of 8,500 California and Arizona citrus growers who supplied their harvests to one of the 115 local Sunkist affiliated packinghouses. The packinghouse, in turn, shipped its fruit solely through channels established by the central Sunkist organization. The packinghouses were members of both a district exchange and Sunkist Growers, Inc.

The third level, the district exchange, would remain a grower-owned cooperative. As it had always done, the district exchange would serve as a regional order fulfillment center for fresh fruit, often for more than one packinghouse. It would be at this level that growers would nominate their representatives to serve as directors of the central Sunkist organization. The number of directors from that district would be based on the volume of fruit handled by its exchange.

75th PLANS PROCEED

Despite the disappointment of the December 1967 freeze, Sunkist refused to disregard its 75th-year anniversary plans for 1968. Although cutbacks in its planned celebrations were made, Sunkist's board of directors insisted that their cooperative's diamond jubilee be properly noted. They believed that Sunkist had achieved a real milestone in business history. The cooperative born out of adversity 75 years earlier received worldwide publicity that year.

ANOTHER FREEZE

But the late Sixties weren't destined to be kind to citrus growers in the Far West. The very next season – 1968-69 – severe weather damage hit the traditional citrus producing areas of Ventura and Orange Counties, the Redlands-Riverside-Corona district, and some areas of the Coachella Valley. An early December freeze caused severe damage but the worst came when unprecedented rainfall, accompanied by heavy flooding and erosion, created a catastrophe. Central California also received damage from cold weather.

"Not since 1913 has the western citrus producing area been so severely damaged by weather," Sunkist reported. "The only applicable description was 'near total disaster' for many growers in many areas."

A DECADE OF CHANGE

Marketing transformations, weather problems and legal troubles had marked the decade of the Sixties. But Sunkist had weathered the problems and maintained its leadership. By entering the international market with new force, the cooperative kept a commanding position in the citrus trade. But through the decade of change, Sunkist had held firm to its original purpose – to market members' fruit and to return to them all proceeds minus the cost of doing business. Whatever else might change, that function never would.

Change was a part of that business, and Sunkist had survived the Sixties not only intact, but ready to take a pro-active stance on coming transitions. As the Sixties closed, Sunkist quietly flexed its strength with the formal opening of its Central California regional headquarters building in Lindsay, California. Reflecting the increasing importance of the San Joaquin Valley's citrus producing volume, the new building would consolidate many of the area activities of Sunkist and its affiliate, the Fruit Growers Supply Company.

The 1930s Sunkist Building at 707 West Fifth Street, once a downtown Los Angeles landmark, was demolished in 1972.

Sunkist introduced its new corporate logo reflecting its marketing and advertising strategy, in 1969.

In 1969, the cooperative would also show its readiness for the future by introducing a new corporate logo for Sunkist Growers, Inc. Designed by Keith N. Thomas and Associates, the new look with its fruit and sprouting leaves ended more than a year of investigation and research to find a logo that reflected Sunkist's new strategy for marketing and advertising.

An even bigger transformation was about to take place.

"After intensive study, your board of directors voted to accept a most attractive offer for the present Sunkist Building from Dillingham Corporation in exchange for a new site in Sherman Oaks, California," general manager Anderson reported in 1969.

Anderson noted that the 35-year-old Sunkist building in downtown Los Angeles was "woefully lacking in space for necessary personnel." The property had declining value. A move was needed.

"Many of us have spent our lives in this building," Anderson observed. ""We will leave with regret but we look with confidence to the future in our new location."

Before Sunkist would leave, the cooperative used its 1969 annual report to pay a photographic tribute to the 1930s Sunkist building at 707 West Fifth Street. That would be Sunkist's last official look at its historic home before it was razed to the ground in 1972.

CHAPTER IX – The 1970s

TRYING TIMES

Construction of Sunkist's new headquarters in Sherman Oaks began in 1969. It marked Sunkist's tenth corporate home since the cooperative's founding in 1893. Located 14 miles from Sunkist's downtown Los Angeles site, it was built by the William Simpson Construction Co., which had erected the previous Sunkist building 35 years before.

The opening of the new Sunkist headquarters in Sherman Oaks symbolized the optimism with which the Seventies began. Located 14 miles from downtown Los Angeles, the new building stood in the San Fernando Valley – once a major citrus producing area whose groves had long since disappeared. Sunkist's new building was three stories tall, encompassed 164,100 square feet and housed an inner courtyard. It had been designed by Albert C. Martin & Associates.

The new site marked the tenth corporate home of the cooperative since its beginning in 1893. And, as before, it also housed the headquarters of the Fruit Growers Supply Company. In the move from the 35-year-old building in downtown Los Angeles, Sunkist brought with it, among other things, the huge murals which had adorned the board room walls of its old office. These were relocated onto the board room walls of the new building on Riverside Drive.

Sunkist also brought to Sherman Oaks its world-renowned name, high quality standards, premium pricing, and a nearly 80-year history as the voice of the Far West citrus grower. After the upheavals of the Sixties, it seemed Sunkist was certainly able to face whatever the Seventies might hold.

This was the prevailing mood, not just for Sunkist and its members, but for American agriculture as a whole. There was a "come back to your senses" mood prevailing in America. People were turning away from the plastic, the unreal and the artificial. "Natural" was quickly becoming a catchword. This atmosphere offered a natural marketing opportunity for Sunkist to promote its fresh, wholesome oranges and lemons.

"In the very early Seventies, every sign seemed to point to expansion," Sunkist's Curt Anderson would later say. "There appeared to be limitless opportunities for growth through foreign trade. Conditions around the world were such that the American farmer was able to sell just about all he could produce and make a very good profit."

At home, a strong U.S. economy helped feed domestic demand. Farmers planted fence-row to fence-row. Improved technology and ideal weather would push production – not just of citrus but all major crops – to record levels. Credit was plentiful and easy. With rising land values, farmers found it advantageous to borrow heavily. They bought new equipment and more land, intending to pay back cheap dollars against ever-increasing crop prices. Inflation took care of risk because farmers could always re-finance, based on their increased paper equity in land. And naturally, rapid inflation also meant additional borrowing was needed to cover annual production expenses.

"It seemed the boom times would go on forever," Anderson said. But they wouldn't.

PREPARING FOR ABUNDANT CROPS

A few insiders, like Sunkist general manager Don Anderson, were already well aware as the decade opened what hurdles lay before the citrus industry. Record growth, change and a myriad of new environmental concerns were apparent.

"As we begin the decade of the 1970s, acreage planted at a record-setting pace in the early 1960s is coming into full bearing," forewarned Sunkist general manager D.M. Anderson, "and the bumper crops we have talked about for so long are no longer just eventualities to be faced at some time in the future."

To prepare to sell these large crops, Sunkist created Sunkist Growth Opportunity Division, or SunGro, in 1970. This endeavor would seek to develop new uses for citrus, new citrus products and new packaging ideas.

As a further expansion step to handle the expected abundance of citrus, Sunkist's orange products division completed construction in 1970 of a multi-million-dollar processing building in Ontario. Old Building #12, built in 1926, was demolished to make room for the more contemporary plant.

The new Ontario facility, sitting on 25 acres, would allow greater manufacturing capacities and diversification in both products and services. In fact, it was designed to process one million tons of citrus products a year, compared to the 200,000 tons averaged yearly through the early Sixties. It would house administrative and management offices, both cold and ambient storage, and a truck station with ample dock space for receiving materials and supplies. It boasted a new 60,000 square-foot freezer warehouse, and two new 1,500-ton silos for storing dried meal to aid in cattle feed marketing.

"All these new installations and equipment were added with a view toward helping solve the modern problems of ecology," reported Anderson, "while making positive contributions to efficiency and performance."

CITRUS GROVES IN TRANSITION

Meanwhile, Sunkist's membership was continuing to evolve, its changes reflecting a trend throughout American agriculture. Growers were decreasing in number while their per-capita acreage amounts were increasing. There were fewer producers handling larger volumes of citrus.

By the mid-1970s, the once flourishing citrus industry of Southern California communities like Pomona was no more. Where once acres and acres of citrus groves and packinghouses had stood, there now were houses. There was virtually no citrus grown anymore in Los Angeles County. In fact, the site of the first commercial grove planted in the 1840s had become the downtown area of Los Angeles, a city that occupied 50,000 acres of urban sprawl by 1977.

The small family citrus grove was making way for the large corporate farming structure, particularly in the new citrus growing areas of Central California and the California and Arizona desert regions. Sunkist's grower relations department worked closely with these entities to orient them to the benefits of having Sunkist market their fruit.

By the late Seventies, a new breed of citrus producer was also beginning to emerge. Attracted by favorable tax laws, which included investment tax credits and generous depreciation allowances, outside investors began to buy up citrus acreage. Syndications, limited partnerships, and big corporations were entering the citrus business, eager to undertake both the producing and marketing of citrus. Sunkist began to see a decline in its membership, as more and more acreage was lost to tax-driven investors. This decline would continue into the Eighties before Sunkist found a way to reverse it.

There were many variations in member-growers' conditions as the Seventies advanced, and it was impossible to generalize about the individual situation of Sunkist's 8,000 members. Higher costs and larger crops had become a way of life, with inflation becoming one of the most serious problems. Labor, fuel, electricity, and fertilizer costs would continue to increase sharply.

Sunkist could not guarantee equal success to all of its members. Yet hard as it was to generalize about California and Arizona's citrus growers, it was still safe to say they produced a valuable commodity. Far West citrus growers still managed to produce 90 percent of the lemons consumed in America and 30 percent of the world's lemon production. Even though California produced only 25 percent of America's oranges, California accounted for more than two-thirds of all oranges consumed fresh.

It was obvious that many growers in the Seventies were facing a period of reckoning. They would be caught between escalating production costs and the suppressed prices that were soon to result from surpluses and economic troubles. Those who were strong enough would survive. The rest would not.

NEWMAN, UTKE MOVE TO THE TOP

Inside Sunkist, changes also were in the making. Milton M. Teague had retired from the board presidency in December 1971 after six years as Sunkist's chief board officer and 22 years as a member of the board of directors.

His replacement would be Ventura's John V. Newman, and the top spot on the board would now be called "chairman." Newman had first been elected to Sunkist's board in 1958, representing the Ventura County Citrus Exchange of Santa Paula.

At the same time, general manager Anderson retired from Sunkist after a 40-year career with the cooperative. His replacement was Roy Utke, who had come to Sunkist Growers from the Fruit Growers Supply Company, where he had been general manager since 1967. And now, the chief executive officer's post was called "president."

Under Utke, Sunkist's internal structure was re-organized. Detailed reporting of accountability, budgeting and expenditures control was implemented. A fresh fruit marketing division was created to encompass all fresh fruit sales, sales promotion and media advertising, resulting in a highly coordinated marketing approach. Sunkist also formed a

Ventura citrus producer John V. Newman served two terms as chairman of Sunkist's board of directors: from 1971-77 and from 1982-85.

Roy Utke, Sunkist president from 1971-78, and before that, general manager of Fruit Growers Supply Company from 1967-71.

government affairs division during that 1971-72 season, giving its members an even more unified and powerful voice in local, state, federal, and international government.

The 1971-72 season brought weather problems for nearly every citrus variety, as well as a dock strike. Despite those difficulties, Sunkist moved 66.6 million cartons of fruit that season. The cooperative handled over 72 percent of the Far West citrus crop and brought in over $238 million (F.O.B. returns) on its fresh fruit and some $78.9 million on total products sales. Vast quantities of fruit were diverted to the two products processing plants. That year, too, Sunkist experienced the largest and most successful export season it had ever known. Over 14.5 million cartons were sold abroad at an average F.O.B. return of $3.89 for all varieties.

In 1972, the Fruit Growers Supply Company would close its one remaining lumber mill at Hilt (once there were three), choosing instead to concentrate on managing its forests for sustained yield. That included selling timber to the lumber and paper industries. By 1975, the Supply Company owned 195,000 acres of forest land in Northern California.

THE ENERGY CRISIS OF 1973

It seemed to hit overnight.

All of a sudden, Americans became aware that their cars, their electricity bills, and their nation's economy were heavily dependent on the black gold that was pumped out of the Middle East's oil fields. People lined up their automobiles at gasoline pumps, watching fuel prices triple as the oil-producing countries of the Middle East increased the price of crude petroleum.

"Never before has Sunkist been so directly and profoundly affected by national and international economic forces," Utke reported in 1973. "Inflation, wage and price controls, devaluation and the economic impact of developing scarcities of energy and raw materials – all had undeniable and significant impact."

Energy consciousness soared at Sunkist. Its headquarters in Sherman Oaks underwent a major re-wiring to turn out the lights at night. Car pooling among employees was implemented.

"The impact of the energy crisis, which is both real and serious, will be felt for years to come not only by growers but in all industries related to agriculture," Utke noted.

Nowhere did Sunkist feel the energy crisis more acutely than in its hard-earned export business, where the cost of shipping fruit over thousands of miles had tripled. Expenses of transporting fruit to market increased and accelerated with the growing recognition of serious fuel shortages.

Added to the transportation problem was the domestic railroad phase-out of "ice-bunker" cars in favor of larger but less readily available refrigerated "mechanicals."

Competition among shippers of all perishables for limited rail and truck space resulted in rate increases.

While Sunkist – and all American exporters – were grappling with soaring fuel and freight costs, the cooperative sustained another hard-hitting impact. In Europe, tariff preference arrangements between members of the European Economic Community and several Mediterranean citrus-growing countries began keeping U.S. citrus shippers at a disadvantage.

Viewing the EEC's tariff discounting as illegal trade discrimination, Sunkist complained to the U.S. government which was participating with 100 other nations in multilateral trade negotiations under the General Agreement on Tariffs and Trade (GATT). Sunkist's position was clear: it asked that the California-Arizona citrus industry be able to compete on an equal basis with all other citrus producers in all world markets.

The barriers placed against Sunkist's shipments from California and Arizona struck deep into the cooperative's business. In its troubles with the European Community, millions of cartons of fruit were at stake. In 1975, Europe was purchasing 5.7 million cartons alone of Sunkist fresh valencia oranges. In fact, in the spring of 1973, Sunkist had consummated its first sale of fresh fruit to the Soviet Union. A few months later, it had made its first sale of valencias to Eastern Europe.

PACIFIC RIM ADVANTAGE

Despite fuel shortages and European trade barriers, Sunkist's export market would gain in size and importance through the Seventies. The domestic market would still remain Sunkist's biggest outlet, accounting for 52 million cartons of fresh fruit. But exports represented an ever-growing market. By the mid-Seventies, Sunkist was exporting over 20 million cartons of fresh fruit a year, with more and more of it heading across the Pacific Ocean.

What would help Sunkist, in addition to its own marketing competence, was an ace-in-the-hole of sorts: its location. Sunkist sat on the edge of the Pacific Rim, and increasingly wealthy trading partners on the other side of the ocean were busy buying American food products like California and Arizona citrus. As business with European markets was diminishing, Sunkist was working vigorously to open Asian markets.

As the decade progressed, about 55 percent of Sunkist's exports were heading to the Far East, with Japan and Hong Kong the strongest markets. Sunkist began chartering a weekly shipping service to principle markets in the Orient, providing regular and adequate shipping space, excellent handling conditions, and a substantial freight rate reduction. The results were record high shipments of both lemons and oranges to all trans-Pacific markets. By 1974, Japan was Sunkist's biggest overseas lemon market with 4 million cartons yearly. France remained Sunkist's major European lemon market, accounting for some 1.5 million cartons a year.

The cooperative would also form overseas subsidiaries. SunMac Hawaii, Ltd. was formed in 1973 by Sunkist Growers Inc. with Alister W. Macdonald to provide improved distribution and packaging facilities for fresh citrus and products marketed in Hawaii through Macdonald & Porter. There would also be Sunkist Pacific, Ltd. in Japan, and Sunkist (Europe) S.A.

SUNKIST'S 80th YEAR

More than 700 grower-members attended Sunkist's 80th annual meeting in January 1974 at the Beverly Wilshire Hotel in Los Angeles. Guest speaker was U.S. Secretary of Agriculture Earl Butz. He applauded Sunkist for its "forward-looking, high-principled, soundly businesslike" approach.

That year Sunkist was celebrating "the year of the dollar," and its biggest year ever in total sales. Reaching a record $381.7 million, its sales figure represented an increase of more than 9 percent over the previous year and a 31 percent jump over the average of the five past seasons.

Sunkist would reach record volumes of fruit handled and payments made to members through the early and mid-Seventies. Yet it was this very growth in fruit volume that made marketing so difficult through much of the decade. In 1969-70, the cooperative handled 97.9 million carton-equivalents of both fresh and processed fruit. By the 1974-75 season, that amount had increased to almost 150 million. For much of the decade, the worldwide citrus supply remained far ahead of demand.

Problems worsened whenever the crop was weather-damaged, resulting in blemished fruit or poor eating quality. When that happened, as in the mid-Seventies, the burden fell on the orange and lemon processing divisions to find outlets for the fruit.

During the 1974-75 season, Sunkist's corporate bank borrowings had been strained to their credit limit in order to accommodate an extraordinarily large volume of products fruit receipts and inventories.

With this, as well as the high fuel costs and European trade hurdles, the citrus industry was "experiencing a trying period of transition, change and stress," Utke would acknowledge in 1976.

TAKING STEPS TO COMPETE

Spurred by the ever-larger crops and the marketing challenges they presented, several steps were taken to advance Sunkist's ability to compete in the world market.

Tremendous growth was being seen in the volume handled by Sunkist's products group, under the direction of vice president Russell L. Hanlin. Once the throwaways of California's citrus industry, fruit for processing was opening new doors for Sunkist. By 1975, nearly 1.3 million tons of fruit – or double the previous year's deliveries – made their way into products orange and lemon processing. In 1974, Sunkist had acquired a juice processing plant and cold storage facility in Yuma, Arizona. During the 1974-75 season, its first full year of operation, this Arizona products division processed almost 100,000 tons of oranges and lemons. Functioning as a satellite plant, the Arizona facility processed basic citrus by-products, such as lemon and orange concentrates, cold pressed lemon oil and oil phase essence.

In 1975, the Sunkist Research Center was completed. Previously, Sunkist's research personnel in both its fresh fruit and its products research and development departments had been working in four separate locations, in facilities that were cramped and obsolete. The new 39,000-square-foot building housed 50 engineers, technicians and scientists developing new products, money-making machines, processes, and techniques.

Sunkist's products during 1976-77 set a new record of $115.5 million in sales. Some of that could be attributed to the multi-million-dollar contracts Sunkist continued to win with the U.S. Department of Agriculture to supply frozen concentrated orange juice for the federal school lunch program. Millions of gallons were shipped out from Sunkist's orange products division in Ontario to meet the program's needs.

But as Sunkist continued to search for other uses for its processed products, the cooperative hit upon a revolutionary idea that would eventually earn the company millions of dollars for years to come.

THE START OF A NEW SOURCE OF INCOME

For several years, Sunkist's few trademark licensed agreements – juice drinks, mostly – had been building. But some felt there was far more potential than was being tapped.

"About 1972, I became vice president of our processed products division," recalled Russell Hanlin. "We realized that the Sunkist brand was terribly underutilized in the manufactured products business, and we took a look at what it would take to become a national distributor of Sunkist brand juices, soft drinks, etc. Then we looked at the consumer packaging equipment and factories we would have to acquire to be efficient, the inventories we would have to carry, the regional warehouses around the nation, and the separate sales force that we'd have to employ to get into the frozen and dairy cases in the supermarket.

"The upfront capital investment, we decided, was beyond the interest of our growers," Hanlin said. "So we decided we would simply make a very dramatic expansion of our trademark licensing programs, and use that as a vehicle for selling our ingredients and utilizing our brand for marketing this wider range of products."

That dramatic decision had not been made overnight. Sunkist's board of directors had been reluctant to make the move into product licensing, in much the same way the old Exchange board had been hesitant to put up funds for advertising back in 1907.

Some directors feared that product licensing might mean the demise of the fresh fruit side of the citrus business, which generated most of Sunkist's revenues. Others felt that

Sunkist board members were present at the groundbreaking of Sunkist's new research facility in Ontario. The facility was built in 1975 to develop new citrus products, machines, processes, and techniques.

In the 1970s, Sunkist began licensing the use of its name on high-quality products that used citrus by-products. The royalties earned from the trademark licensing helped lower growers' investment in their cooperative.

putting the Sunkist name on products like soft drinks and candy would dilute the trademark's quality image.

"But we had done marketing research that showed that the consumer made a great distinction between drinking a carbonated soft drink and eating an orange," Hanlin explained years later. "The research showed that if it were a good, high-quality soft drink that the consumer liked, it would not reduce their perception of the quality of Sunkist."

Hanlin's products group had discovered that the Sunkist trademark was greatly underutilized and had enormous potential. In fact, research showed that consumers fully expected that there should be a Sunkist orange soda. "The trademark was naturally tributary to a wide range of citrus products that we were not involved in," Hanlin said.

TRADEMARK LICENSING

With the board's approval, Sunkist began licensing its name in 1974 to Ben Myerson Candy Co., Inc. which sold Sunkist® Fruit Gem candies. Made from fruit jellied pectin, the candies were made from citrus by-products purchased from Sunkist. This not only offered another market for a Sunkist product, but the cooperative received royalty payments for Myerson's use of the trademark. Quality of the candy was stressed, reinforcing the connection to the Sunkist name.

In 1977, an agreement was concluded with General Cinema Corporation, a major independent soft drink bottler and motion picture exhibitor, providing for the marketing of citrus-flavored carbonated drinks bearing the Sunkist trademark. The deal granted General Cinema a license to market Sunkist-trademarked carbonated soft drinks in the U.S. Sunkist would sell the flavoring base used by the franchise bottlers and receive a significant royalty on every case sold.

"Considering the most conservative projections for this new business development," Sunkist president Utke reported at the time, "it appears that millions of dollars of new products sales and royalties will be generated for Sunkist in coming years."

Under General Cinema Corporation, the Sunkist Soft Drinks, Inc. subsidiary began test-marketing the new orange carbonated soft drink bearing the Sunkist name. Spurred by attention-grabbing advertising and packaging, sales results were outstanding.

The 1977-78 season also saw the successful introduction of Sunkist brand juice drinks in Taiwan under a technical assistance and trademark license agreement. A European licensee enjoyed early success with new flavors of BRIK-PAK juices. Licenses in Japan and Hong Kong unleashed elaborate multi-million-dollar media advertising and promotional campaigns to build brand awareness for their beverages and frozen confections sold under the Sunkist trademark.

The Sunkist name had been a registered trademark of the cooperative since 1909. It was vigilantly guarded as one of Sunkist's most valuable assets. Only Sunkist had the right to license the name, although scores of companies and individual entrepreneurs tried to hitch a free ride on the trademark. Whenever Sunkist learned of unauthorized use of its name, it took every legitimate and legal means of protecting it.

That other companies wanted and were allowed to market products under the Sunkist name was proof of the market power of the trademark. All participants in Sunkist's licensing program were carefully screened before being approved, and continually scrutinized by the cooperative to ensure that the products were meeting quality standards.

Not only would trademark licensing create millions of dollars of income for Sunkist and its members, but eventually those royalties would help replace the need for grower investment in the cooperative, although that benefit would not be fully realized for another 10 years.

COOPERATIVES - AND SUNKIST - COME UNDER ATTACK

As the decade progressed, the agricultural scenario began to reflect uncertainty in the face of worldwide and uncontrolled inflation, threatened recession, continued shortages of basic resources, and public mistrust of business and government – this last certainly influenced by the Watergate scandal and the resignation of Richard Nixon from the U.S. Presidency.

Government regulations and paperwork grew in mass and became more complex. Its intervention in operations became more pervasive than ever. And America's farm cooperatives like Sunkist began to come under attack. Consumer groups accused co-ops of being too big and powerful. Critics wondered whether grower-owned organizations posed a threat to fair competition, or whether they were a threat to higher prices. In point of fact, even the very largest co-ops were nowhere as large or powerful as the huge corporations with which they were competing.

The criticisms intensified. As the largest factor in the California-Arizona citrus industry, Sunkist was singled out in the mid-1970s for a direct challenge by the Federal Trade Commission. In 1974, Sunkist was requested to provide information to the Bureau of Competition as part of a broad study of agricultural cooperatives. By the end of that year, the FTC staff published a report criticizing dominant cooperatives as well as marketing orders. Sunkist was officially notified that the Bureau of Competition had begun a law enforcement investigation of the citrus industry.

In 1977, this "watchdog" regulatory agency filed a formal complaint against Sunkist alleging anti-competitive practices, including "undue price enhancement." The FTC alleged that Sunkist had achieved and maintained a monopoly in the western citrus industry through "anticompetitive means." The FTC did not care, perhaps, that the cooperative only handled about 16 percent of the nation's citrus and less than six percent of the world's.

A COOPERATIVE'S DISTINCTIONS

"Basically, all cooperatives – regardless of type – were born out of economic necessity, as a form of self-help, by like-minded people who believed they could obtain goods and services more effectively and economically as a group than they could as individuals.

Standing alone, a farmer lacks bargaining strength and is forced to accept whatever price is offered by buyers – assuming he can locate a buyer. By joining with others in the same plight, a farmer who becomes a member of a cooperative is able to compete with some influence in the marketplace without sacrificing his individual ownership and independent decision-making. He is free to concentrate on what he does best – producing a crop – knowing that his cooperative has on its staff a professional marketing team to sell his crop for the best possible return.

There are a number of widely-held misconceptions about cooperatives. One myth is that cooperatives are exempt from antitrust legislation. Not so. The Capper-Volstead Act simply permits farmers to join together to process, prepare, handle, and sell the farm products of the members and patrons. It permits them to use marketing agencies in common as a means of carrying out these legitimate functions.

In many respects, cooperatives are organized like other businesses and operate in much the same way. But in several significant respects, they differ from other forms of business enterprise. Among these distinctions are:

One, cooperatives are voluntary membership organizations. If, at any time, the member-owners perceive that their cooperative is not operating in their interest or in the public interest, they can initiate program changes, hire new management, form a new organization, or terminate their membership.

Two, cooperatives are governed by democratic process. The members elect representatives to serve on the board of directors. Voting control is based on membership or business done with the cooperative, not on the amount of investment as in a stock corporation.

Three, cooperatives operate on a non-profit, or cost-of-doing-business basis. Economic benefits after expenses are returned to the members or patrons according to their use of the cooperative's services.

Four, the cooperative's members participate in financing their business. Since it is the members who are primarily interested in the success of the business, they must assume the responsibility of providing capital for their cooperative's operations.

Five, cooperatives foster free enterprise by allowing members to exercise their own initiative. Farm operators who market their crops or buy their supplies cooperatively still react individually to market price signals in making their production decisions. If prices ever become artificially high, farmers will respond with increased production to take advantage of the good market. That increased production will, in turn, pressure market prices back down again. With supply and demand in balance, consumers enjoy plentiful supplies of food at reasonable prices.

In short, farmer cooperatives play a vital economic role in contributing to the celebrated efficiency of American agriculture.... Though farmer cooperatives are under direct attack by some who would make drastic changes in this form of doing business, we at Sunkist Growers, Inc. believe that the unique characteristics of cooperatives make their continued growth clearly in the public interest. We are confident that these organizations will not only survive the challenges facing them, but will continue to thrive as a most dynamic element of America's private enterprise economy."

- Sunkist Growers, Inc., 1978

"We can only conclude that the FTC complaint actually represents an attack on all cooperatives in the country," Utke said. "Either that, or there is a complete lack of knowledge on the part of the FTC staff as to how cooperatives function."

Sunkist responded with a vigorous defense, denying any violation of law and challenging many of the factual allegations. The cooperative also contested the jurisdiction of the FTC. Sunkist maintained that its purpose – and that of all other agricultural marketing cooperatives – was "quite simple and . . .impossible to fault: namely to achieve a fair return to growers while maintaining consistent supplies of quality food to consumers at reasonable prices."

The suit would take four years and cost Sunkist members millions of dollars before it was resolved.

LIMITATIONS

While the FTC was battling Sunkist, the cooperative continued to have its own major battles in the marketplace. The huge citrus crops coming out of the groves of California and Arizona meant Sunkist had to sell more and more fruit. It meant new markets to open, new horizons and constantly increasing expectations. In fact, in June 1974, Sunkist had shipped a record-breaking one million cartons of fresh fruit in a single week through the Port of Long Beach.

Even for Sunkist, it was hard trying every year to surpass the one before it.

"The 1975-76 season was a pivotal, transitional year for Sunkist because it was the first recent year in which those high expectations were not really met," President Utke reported.

That year Sunkist experienced a setback in sales, falling to $452.3 million from $482.9 the year before. Problems centered on the volume of fruit produced, how and where to sell it, how to process it, how to finance the costs.

Not every grower made money through those years. But, in those years of oversupply, of change, of stress, Sunkist offered growers a home for their fruit, just as it had done back in 1893.

"Neither Sunkist nor any other marketing organization can guarantee a profit for every grower every year," noted Utke. "But we believe that year in and year out, Sunkist provides the best package of marketing services in the citrus business. And in a period of oversupply and competition, Sunkist should continue to average well ahead of the rest of the industry because of our reservoir of marketing and experience."

TURNAROUND

Caught in the FTC complaint case, and now recognizing the impact of government on business, the cooperative's board of directors established a Sunkist Political Action Com-

FROM THE GROWER'S POINT OF VIEW

Top left: "I'm a believer in cooperative marketing. I've been a member of Sunkist since 1934, except for one year. In 1936, I think it was, a friend with a packinghouse in Phoenix said he could get me more money. But at the end of the season, when I got my check, it was almost nothing! I decided maybe the Sunkist organization wasn't so bad after all, and I was right back on my former packinghouse doorstep, asking to rejoin."

- Walter White, Mesa, Arizona, 1977

Bottom left: "When farmers do battle in the political arena, the losers outnumber the winners. But someone has to get in there and fight. . . . What really disturbs me is that I see our basic freedoms being undermined. I think the Federal Trade Commission's complaint against Sunkist is actually an attack on all farmer cooperatives and a threat to our free enterprise system. No one forces me to belong to a co-op. But if the FTC or anyone else ever succeeds in undermining or limiting the option growers have of forming cooperatives, then they would be making a very important business decision affecting my farm. Freedom of choice is very precious to me. . ."

- Dave Kelley, Hemet, California, 1977
(now a California State Senator)

Right: "I have always kept the ranch in Sunkist. I've seen other packers come and go, promising great things to growers. But they can't deliver year after year. Sunkist has kept this industry alive. So much of the industry's production is by growers with small farms, working together. We must all work together to survive."

- T. Allen Lombard, Rancho Sespe,
Ventura County, California, 1977

mittee in 1978. The Sunkist P.A.C. would solicit funds from member-growers and make contributions to election campaigns of leaders sympathetic to the needs of agriculture and citrus growers as well as understanding of their problems.

Sunkist had other responses to the trying times of the Seventies. Just before the end of the 1977-78 season, the trademark stamp appearing on all premium quality fruit marketed by Sunkist was re-designed. The new stamp would incorporate the original Sunkist typeface with the company's easily recognized corporate logo (the fruit shape with a stem and two leaves). This new identification clearly set SUNKIST® apart from competing look-alike brands and allowed retailers to effectively capitalize on the overwhelming consumer preference for Sunkist's citrus.

Internally, there were changes too. Sunkist's board had seen John V. Newman complete his five-year term as chairman in 1977, and David I. Kline of Visalia take over the board's top spot. Newman would, like Harvey A. Lynn and Milton M. Teague before him, become Chairman of the Board, Emeritus. (In March 1979, Lynn died at the age of 95. Teague passed away in 1986 at 83.)

Marketing and management differences with president Utke, particularly with regard to exports, had led marketing vice president Robert Autenreith to leave the organization in 1976 to form his own company. (Tragically, Autenreith and his wife would be killed in a car accident in 1984.)

Two years later, in the summer of 1978, similar marketing and management issues caused Utke to resign from Sunkist. Utke would move on into the construction business.

HANLIN BECOMES PRESIDENT

The board of directors soon found Utke's replacement. He would be Russell L. Hanlin, a 27-year-employee then serving as vice president of Sunkist's products group. Hanlin could be called an American success story, having risen through the ranks from mail clerk to president of the organization.

Not long after Hanlin took over the helm, two severe freezes struck both California and Arizona, first in December 1978 and then again in January 1979. Hit most strongly was Sunkist's products group, which received only 60 percent of the volume it normally would have taken in. Operations at the processing plant in Corona were sharply curtailed, and hundreds of employees were laid off. Many growers suffered the loss of a significant portion of an already small crop.

The smaller crop produced 54 million cartons, almost 20 percent below the previous year's crop and more than 24 percent below the prior three-year average. Yet the 1978-79 season would prove to be successful as Sunkist put its sophisticated and resourceful marketing abilities to work. The average carton of fresh citrus fruit handled by Sunkist that

Visalia's David I. Kline, Sunkist chairman of the board from 1977-82.

Russell L. Hanlin has served as president of Sunkist Growers since 1978.

season increased in value by almost 30 percent over 1977-78 prices. Sunkist's total sales during that freeze-affected season of 1978-79 reached an all-time high of $611.9 million.

The freeze helped put to the test Sunkist's new electro-mechanical grader (EMG), which had finally become commercially available after ten years of research. The system was considered revolutionary, and could effectively grade both the external and internal quality characteristics of citrus fruit. It employed low-level X-ray and electronic processes to detect flaws.

RESUMING THE PACE

Despite the trying times of the decade, Sunkist had continued to grow. Sunkist's total sales had grown by almost 50 percent between 1973 and 1979. By the last season of the decade, Sunkist's trademark licensing program involved agreements with products manufacturers in 16 nations in Europe, the Far East, the Middle East, Canada, and the U.S. Sales of ingredients for use in licensed products exceeded $7.8 million, in addition to royalty payments for the use of the Sunkist trademark.

Sunkist now had 6,500 ranches in California and Arizona signed into its membership, ranging in size from five acres to as high as 10,000. If the grower-owners of those ranches were counted, there were actually some 15,000 people comprising Sunkist's ownership. These included husbands and wives as well as business partnerships, all considered "the backbone of the organization."

The cooperative had 37 fresh fruit sales offices around the country. By-products were sold through its Products Sales Divisions in Ontario, California and Englewood Cliffs, New Jersey. Its products processing plants were located in Yuma, Arizona, and Ontario and Corona, California. It held three overseas subsidiaries. There were some 1,800 Sunkist employees in sales, processing, research, field activities and administration in various locations around the world.

The pivotal Seventies had clearly shown to the economy and businesses of America that the marketplace was now global. Any business expecting to stay in the game in the Eighties would have to enter the international playing field. Sunkist had now positioned itself for strength in that global arena. But the cooperative could hardly know then, as the Seventies closed, that the biggest challenges of the Eighties would lie in its own backyard.

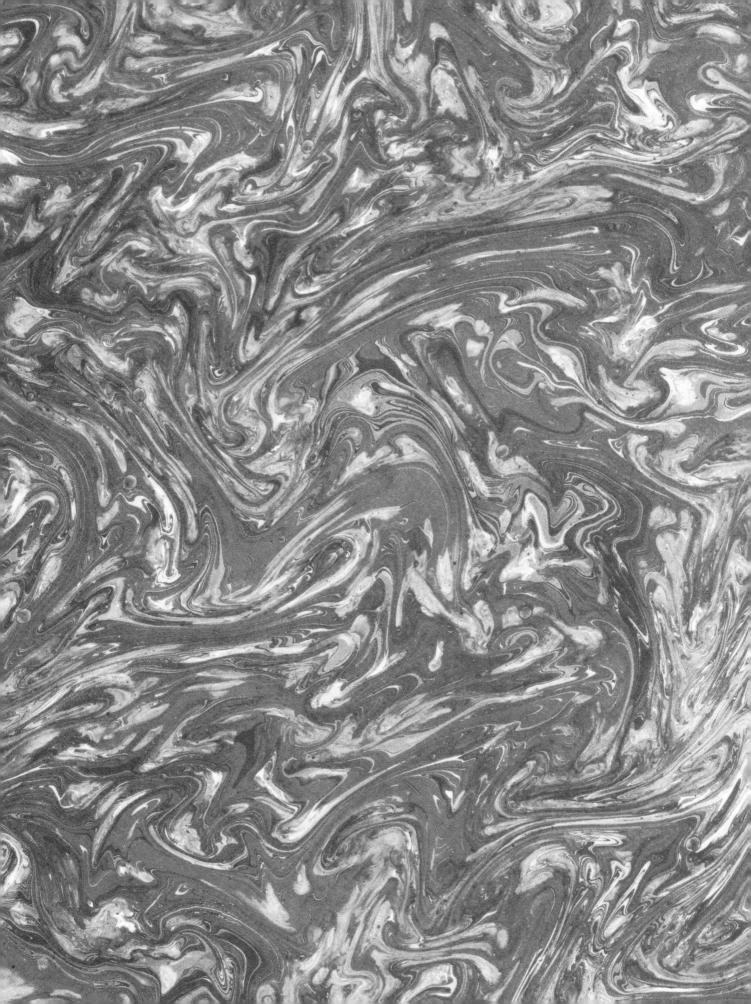

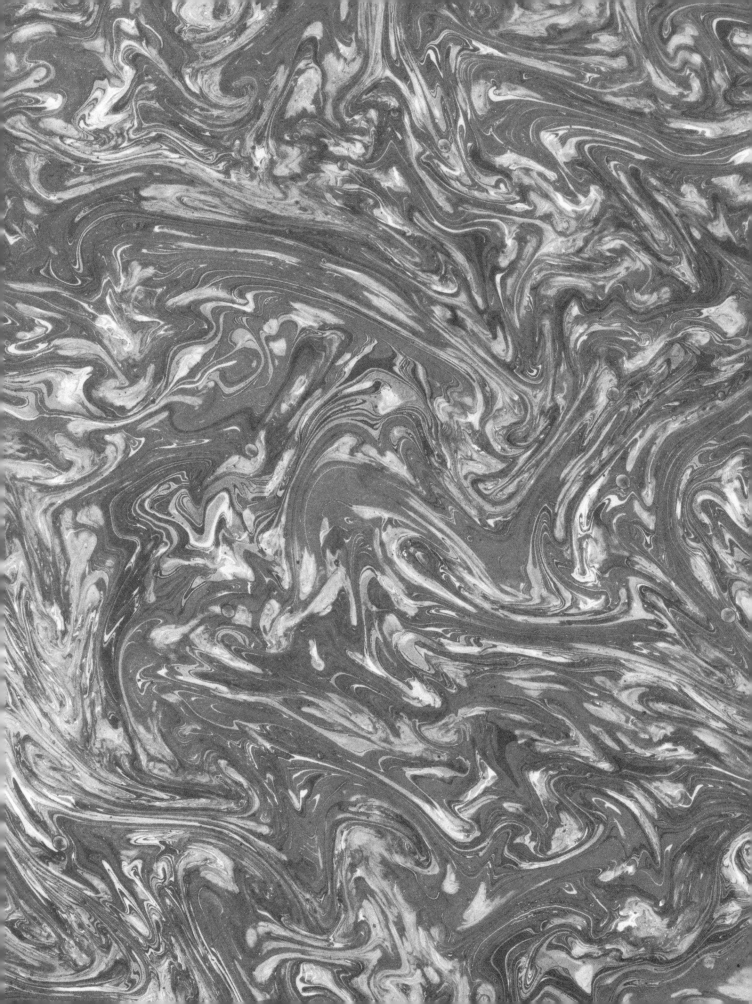

CHAPTER X – The 1980s

CRISES ON THE HOME FRONT

The early Eighties marked an abrupt change in the economic environment for U.S. farmers. Global demand for U.S. agricultural exports plummeted, weakened by financial instability in a number of countries, a stronger U.S. dollar, losses related to the 1980 U.S. embargo on grain sales to the Soviet Union, and the continued political and trade tensions around the world.

There were other problems too: high energy costs, record-high interest rates and ongoing concerns of a potential energy shortage. During the late 1970s, inflation had caused the value of the dollar to decline dramatically. But by the early 1980s, the value of the dollar had risen some 30 percent over the currency values of other countries. Interest rates hit 21 percent.

Finally, farmers suffered several successive years of terrible weather, especially in the American Midwest. Land values deflated. In the ensuing cash-flow "crunch," there were increasing numbers of delinquencies, foreclosures and bankruptcies. With farmers strained financially, many farm-related business, including cooperatives, were affected.

While these national and international problems also affected Sunkist and its members, perhaps the cooperative's most keenly-felt crises of the Eighties occurred on its California-Arizona home front. The decade would bring unprecedented controversy over marketing orders and a public outcry over agriculture's attempts to battle the "Medfly." These battles would be fought, as never before, on the front pages and television screens of the news media.

DECLINE IN MEMBERSHIP

But most worrisome to Sunkist was the decline in its membership. In the 1960s, its membership share had reached almost 80 percent of the Far West citrus crop. By the 1982-83 season, that share had eroded to 56 percent.

Much of this decline could be attributed to the arrival of the big syndicates and corporations in the citrus business. Before the 1970s, nearly 100 percent of California and Arizona's citrus groves had belonged to smaller family farmers. But substantial changes were being seen in the structure of the California-Arizona citrus industry. The amount of syndicated land deals had increased. By the 1980s, several commercial firms had emerged in the Western citrus industry who could advance cash to growers or purchase their crops in the field. The industry began to see the entry of large business conglomerates who tied growers to them through loans and advances.

By the early 1980s, Sunkist's membership had dropped to 5,000. The number of growers who retained independence in their marketing decision-making declined, while the amount of "captive" acreage increased.

Against this background of eroding market share, Sunkist took a look at its priorities, and dramatically revised them. It made massive cost reductions in the organization. More importantly, it decided it had to reduce the capital fund requirement for grower-members.

BREAKING THE MEMBERSHIP BARRIER

In many ways, Sunkist growers' investment in their company had become a barrier to the cooperative's membership. As in all cooperatives, Sunkist's capital fund was financed by retaining a small percentage of grower returns for a specified period. (Sunkist members were also making two other investments in their marketing association: one, for general administrative and marketing programs, which provided the funds to operate Sunkist's marketing system, and the other, for advertising and promotion to fund international, national, and local image building.)

The capital fund allowed Sunkist to build factories and offices, to purchase furnishings and equipment and provided funds to partially carry its products inventories. The growers' investment had been employed on a six-year revolving cycle. At the end of six years, these retains were returned in full to members, although without any accrued interest. One of the biggest drawbacks was that members had to pay income tax on the assessment in the year it was retained, rather than in the year it was revolved back to the grower.

By the early 1980s, growers' capital assessments amounted to 2 cents per carton on fresh fruit; its requirements on processed products totaled $7.50 per ton on lemons and $5.50 per ton on all other processed varieties. With the double digit inflation and high interest rates of the early Eighties, as well as the tax consequences, Sunkist's assessment hit growers with a double whammy. This punitive investment was restricting Sunkist membership.

When its capital investment fund rose to $55 million, and its borrowings reached $100 million in the late 1970s and early 1980s, Sunkist's board and management began to seek a way to bring down members' outlay in their organization.

They would find it in their organization's own name – specifically, in the revenue the Sunkist trademark was earning through the soft drink license arrangement and other outside business programs. In the 1978-79 season, Sunkist had realized $4.7 million – significantly exceeding expectations – from such arrangements. Due to the phenomenal royalties these trademark licensing programs were earning, the cooperative decided to use this income to substantially decrease the capital investment for its members.

By 1980, the downsizing on capital requirements had begun. By 1984, the revolving-fund cycle was shortened to five years. Assessments were cut to just 53 cents per ton on all varieties for processing, and to a mere 1 cent per carton on fresh fruit. In all, Sunkist's capital fund requirements would decrease by an astonishing 90 percent from their highs.

And it was all made possible by Sunkist's licensing income, which earned the cooperative millions of dollars every year. In addition to the tremendously successful licensing programs for the orange soda and Fruit Gems, Sunkist had also signed an agreement with the Thomas J. Lipton Company in 1980 for juices and fruit confections. In 1983 alone, Sunkist realized $10 million in trademark royalties. These supplemental revenues enabled the cooperative to reduce its members' capital fund assessments repeatedly.

At the same time, Sunkist's equity would grow substantially. In fact, in time, Sunkist would be able to distribute the supplemental income directly to members. This, of course, helped the cooperative generate substantially better earnings for its members than independent marketers.

The cooperative also profited from the Northern California timberland maintained by the Fruit Growers Supply Company. All brought in incremental revenue for Sunkist growers.

FTC CASE COMES TO AN END

In June 1980, an agreement had been reached between Sunkist and the Federal Trade Commission in settling the "citrus industry monopolization" complaint issued by the government agency some three-and-a-half years before.

Approved by the Sunkist board of directors, the agreement specially included an acknowledgment that it was not an admission of any unlawful activity by the cooperative.

Terms of the settlement called for Sunkist to divest itself of its $4-million processing plant in Yuma, Arizona. (This would not be achieved until 1984.) Sunkist was not to acquire any existing citrus processing facilities in California or Arizona for ten years without prior FTC approval. The cooperative would also be required to limit the total number of affiliated commercial licensed packing facilities to 39 for five years, and to refrain from direct packinghouse ownership for the same period, without prior FTC approval.

At the time of the agreement, Sunkist did not own any citrus packinghouses, and there were only 37 affiliated commercial packing facilities. "The fact that we had gone 90 years without owning packinghouses made these concessions irrelevant but it made it appear that we had agreed to something substantive," Sunkist president Hanlin would later say. "In retrospect, if I had to do it over again, I wouldn't even have given them that. But when you're spending $3 million year after year in legal defenses and all you have to do is sell a $4 million factory to stop the bleeding, you do it."

The case had cost Sunkist members millions of dollars. It had required attorneys hundreds of hours to peruse thousands of documents. More than 10 years later, the case still rankled Hanlin. He had become president of Sunkist a year after the FTC suit was filed, and had watched it unfold.

"I can remember years when we had every conference room in this building occupied by document classifiers," Hanlin recalled. "They subpoenaed 17 years of Sunkist records. It was unbelievable – a multi-million dollar cost to the company that went on for years. Finally, their case collapsed on them, which was a disgrace.

Top: Aerial spraying of malathion in the 1980s helped combat the medfly's serious threat to the state's billion-dollar agricultural industry. But the spraying drew outcries as the public worried about possible danger from the insecticide.   Bottom left: Traps serve as the first warning of a possible Mediterranean fruit fly infestation.   Bottom right: After Japan announced fumigation requirements on all medfly hosts in the early 1980s, Sunkist quickly designed a shipboard fumigation procedure that enabled its important export shipments to continue without lengthy delays.

167

"They wasted tens of millions of dollars of American resources, based on nothing more than the revisionist ideas of a couple of misguided bureaucrats. 'Trial by theory' is the most un-American thing I have ever experienced," Hanlin concluded.

MEDFLY ALARM

On June 5, 1980, the trapping of an adult Mediterranean fruit fly in the San Fernando Valley signaled the beginning of the first truly serious infestation in California. The pest was considered one of the worst enemies to citrus.

The outbreak alarmed not only citrus growers but producers of other fruits and vegetables. An attack by the voracious Medfly could cause losses of millions of dollars worth of fruit, as well as the possible closures of markets like Japan, which feared a spread of the infestation to their countries.

An eradication program of releasing sterile Medflies was immediately put into place. The outbreak was declared under control by December, and California's fruit and vegetable industry thought its problems with the Medfly were over.

It was wrong.

In May 1981, a crisis occurred. Hundreds of fertile fruit fly and larval finds were made in the Bay area. The Governor of California, Jerry Brown, "ignored the predetermined trigger for aerial spraying and 12 precious days were wasted in combating the spread of the pest," Sunkist reported. "Twelve days are critical in dealing with a pest that goes through an entire life cycle in 24 days during the summer."

Another outbreak was discovered in Los Angeles. Although brought under quick control, the massive attention it received heightened both consumer and trade fears, and helped lead to a Japanese quarantine of food products from the entire state of California.

Ironically, the Medfly infestation remained distant from all commercial citrus growing areas.

The Japanese government soon announced it would require fumigation of all Medfly host fruits and vegetables. Sunkist research and development staff quickly designed and built fumigation facilities, then perfected a shipboard fumigation procedure. The quarantine was lifted in June 1982.

But the Medfly controversy would continue beyond the 1980s. Vocal opponents of the malathion sprayed by helicopters over Los Angeles to combat the Medfly drew front-page media attention. While California agriculture fought to protect its billion-dollar industry from Mother Nature's Medfly infestation, the chasm between the state's urban and rural interests widened ever further.

ATTACK ON MARKETING ORDERS

The navel orange crop of 1980-81 broke all volume records, reaching some 78 million cartons compared to a normal 58 million. Yet much of the fruit was so abnormally small, it could not be handled either in fresh fruit markets or by commercial juice extractors. The only alternative was diverting some of the low-quality early-season navels to cattle feeding, "where at least the cost of handling was recoverable," Hanlin reported. Marketing order opponents tried to paint the picture in the minds of the nation's news media that the cooperative was dumping fruit.

Competitors in the citrus industry, "with their own interests in mind," Sunkist said, decried the use of federal marketing orders, and used the tumultuous marketing period as a springboard to attack the system of orderly distribution.

The outcry resulted in an investigation of marketing orders by the Vice President's Task Force on Regulatory Reform, as well as probes by the U.S. Department of Agriculture, the Office of Management and Budget, and Congress.

Since the 1930s, the California-Arizona citrus industry had used marketing orders that utilized a flow-to-market feature, or "prorate" provision. Under this system, an industry committee, nominated by the growers and appointed by the U.S. Secretary of Agriculture, determined the amount of fruit that could be absorbed into the domestic market each week without gluts or shortages. The rest was then channeled into export outlets or diverted to processed products.

During the summer of 1981, a major federal hearing on the Navel Orange Marketing Order was held in Exeter, California. "A defense led by the government affairs division of Sunkist and the California- Arizona Citrus League proved the validity and the importance of that order," Hanlin reported.

In October, a grower referendum was held to determine whether or not the marketing order should be continued. A full 91 percent of participating navel growers voted in favor of the marketing order.

"Astonishingly, despite these victories," Hanlin said, "the unscrupulous attack on marketing orders continues. . . and pressure continues to be exerted from within the Department of Agriculture."

Attacks on marketing orders continued as bumper crops increased the difficulty of citrus marketing and led to depressed prices. It seemed most observers had forgotten why the prorate system had been devised to begin with. Few people remembered the troublesome surpluses during the Thirties before prorate was implemented, or C.C. Teague's radio talks which explained why marketing orders worked to the benefit of both grower and consumer.

Sunkist continued to present its side of the controversy, and worked to keep it in accurate perspective.

"From year to year, nature produces massive variations in agricultural production," Hanlin explained. "Merely adequate plantings result in shortages each time there is a small crop. Any nation which expects to feed its population and supply its markets every day of the year must produce to the point of surplus in all but the low crop years.

"Surplus causes bankruptcy for farmers," continued the Sunkist executive. "Therefore, to encourage a constant production of abundance, our national agricultural policy includes a series of programs designed to protect farmers from the economic consequences of surplus. In most cases, this takes the form of direct subsidies with tax dollars.

"During 1983 alone, our government spent more than $30 billion on the PIK (Payment-In-Kind) program, target prices, parity and federal purchases of surplus commodities. But when we consider the quantity, quality and price of food we enjoy, there is no question that we, as citizens, benefit from these programs. However, citrus growers do not receive a single dollar of these support funds.

"Instead, we rely upon marketing orders to sensibly deal with supply problems," Hanlin added. "In democratic elections, which require the approval of the vast majority of the producers in the industry, farmers are allowed to implement marketing orders to manage supply. It seems much more noble for producers to exercise this self-restraint, rather than have government purchase surplus at the direct expense of taxpayers."

Despite this rational explanation, marketing order controversy would continue to consume much of Sunkist's time for the rest of the decade.

SUNKIST CHALLENGES USDA ON MARKETING ORDERS

Marketing orders would once more make front-page news when, in April 1984, the U.S. Department of Agriculture – much to Sunkist's astonishment – issued a decision proposing 22 amendments to the orange marketing order. In Sunkist's view, several of the amendments where actually disguised means to deprive the cooperative of a reasonable voice in future marketing decisions. The amendments were offered to growers in an unprecedented type of referendum wherein their only choice was to approve all 22 changes or vote marketing orders out of existence.

"It is clear this occurred only because a handful of dissidents convinced a few strategically-positioned government officials that they speak for the majority of growers in this industry, including a great many Sunkist growers," an angry Hanlin noted.

In response to the alarming marketing order situation, Sunkist's 24-member board of directors took intrepid action. It voted unanimously to use its lawful power – as the elected representatives of the cooperative's more than 5,000 members – to bloc vote for Sunkist growers. The directors boldly signaled their intent to effectively vote the orders out of existence unless the government restored to growers a reasonable choice in the referendum.

Immediately after the Sunkist board's vote, a delegation of Sunkist board members and management traveled to Washington, D.C. to present its complaints to key members of Congress and to U.S. Secretary of Agriculture John Block. Congress urged the Secretary to reconsider his "Hobson's Choice" method of voting. "To his credit, he did," Sunkist would later report.

The earlier decision was modified to allow growers to vote on the individual amendments without the continuation of the orders being in jeopardy. As a result, Sunkist's board of directors rescinded its bloc vote and encouraged every Sunkist grower to exercise his or her best judgment on the individual issues.

The referendum was held, with 94 percent of participating growers voting for the continuation of the marketing order.

BLUEPRINT FOR THE FUTURE

Since Sunkist had first begun witnessing the changes the 1980s were bringing to the agricultural and business scene, it had sought ways to cope with them. Aggressive responses from the cooperative would prove to be the right answer.

In addition to lowering its capital fund requirement, Sunkist had developed a blueprint for the future, "a plan that will assure a brighter prospect for current and future members of this cooperative," President Hanlin reported.

The blueprint involved important changes in fresh fruit sales operations, both domestic and export. This involved, among other things, an improved communications system with better access to Sunkist's central sales operations and computer-monitored inventories for up-to-date information.

As part of this aggressive strategy, Sunkist would adopt a new plan for its processed products inventory. The Just-In-Time program of quick-response sales and lower inventories was implemented at Sunkist, helping reduce massive stocks of product that were being carried at painfully high interest rates. In turn, this helped lower Sunkist's borrowings needed to carry its inventory, and return earnings to grower-members faster than ever before.

The plan also involved a complete restructuring of Sunkist's products group. In 1980, Sunkist announced that it planned to dispose of its Corona property, where the Lemon Products division had been located since 1916. The Corona plant had borne a tremendous cost burden as the only citrus processing facility in the nation required to construct and operate a massive waste water treatment plant. This was largely the result of the population growth that had transformed Corona from a small industrial center surrounded by groves to a residential city of considerable size.

Many of the Corona buildings were old, some as many as 50 years old, making them obsolete and ineffective. And the focus of citrus production had shifted from Southern California to Central California and Arizona. Hauling fruit the 200-mile distance from the San Joaquin Valley – over a range of mountains – to Corona and Ontario had become ex-

Fruit Growers Supply Company began manufacturing corrugated cartons in 1979 at its new plant in Ontario, Calif. State-of-the-art equipment made it one of the world's most efficient manufacturing facilities.

tremely expensive. Crude oil costs had risen over 1000 percent since 1973 and transporting products fruit long distances was no longer cost effective.

With the significant increase in the value of the Corona property, Sunkist could relocate to another California site without further capital investment from its grower-members.

Sunkist would begin construction on a new processing plant in 1981 near Tipton in Central California – now a major citrus producing region. It would be completed by the next year. Additional equipment was installed in Sunkist's processing plant in Ontario, California to expand its capabilities to process all citrus varieties.

The Fruit Growers Supply Company also continued to advance with the times to offer cost-effective supplies for Sunkist members. In November 1979, it had begun producing Sunkist cartons at its new container manufacturing plant in Ontario. The capabilities of the new, highly automated plant resulted in a substantial savings per carton for Sunkist members. And through the 1980s, the Supply Company would allocate millions of dollars to its members from the after-tax earnings primarily from its timberland operations.

Despite bumper crops that often depressed prices, Sunkist managed to record higher and higher revenues during the Eighties. Its payments to growers, after operational costs, also reached record levels. For the 1981-82 season, sales totaled $683.4 million, and payments to growers reached $489.4 million. That year, navels brought the highest F.O.B. prices ever for a non-freeze year – $6.71 average per carton compared to $5.23 the previous year. Even with a worldwide surplus, lemons brought in an average of $9.02 (F.O.B.) per carton.

In 1982, Ventura's John V. Newman had once again been elected Sunkist's chairman of the board. He took over from David I. Kline, the statesman-like, Harvard-educated farmer who was the first chairman elected from the San Joaquin Valley.

And in 1983, Sunkist marked 75 years of continuous advertising with its agency, Foote, Cone & Belding (long ago known as Lord & Thomas).

SUNKIST FOCUSES ON REAL ESTATE

In the 1980s atmosphere of industry shake-up, Sunkist had realized that maintaining a large volume base was absolutely essential. The cooperative was working hard to ease membership requirements and to upgrade its operations, but helping growers and packinghouses hold onto their properties was another matter.

In April 1984, Sunkist lost a big chunk of membership when five Sunkist-affiliated commercial packinghouses owned by Blue Goose Growers, Inc., an agribusiness corporation, were unexpectedly sold outright to Castle & Cooke, another agribusiness firm eager to gain a foothold in California citrus. The five packing facilities involved several hundred Sunkist member-growers and some ten percent of the company's volume base.

To help grower-members finance land purchases, Sunkist and Fruit Growers Supply Co. organized Sunkist Real Estate, Inc. in 1988. The new company helped Sunkist maintain its volume base by attracting additional citrus acreage and retaining acreage already in the system.

In response, Sunkist immediately stepped up its member relations activities. Within the year, the cooperative had successfully relocated 30 percent of those growers with other Sunkist-affiliated packinghouses. That season, Sunkist also signed four new affiliated shippers into its membership, which meant that the organization would enter 1985 with its overall membership only marginally changed.

By the fall of 1987, the number of grower memberships recovered had reached 50 percent. New packinghouse affiliates had grown to eight. At the same time, several packers had dropped by the wayside, but overall, Sunkist had gained more than it had lost.

Yet again, two more Sunkist commercial packinghouses – one a Sunkist affiliate for 40 years – were purchased by the same buyer. This time, 250 growers were affected. Most of those with the freedom to relocate moved to another Sunkist packinghouse.

But this second selling maneuver had been quite disconcerting. Throughout the period, Sunkist's performance had remained superior to its competition. Why hadn't that been enough?

Sunkist officials recognized that a substantial part of the cooperative's effectiveness could be attributed to the decision by the majority of the industry's growers and shippers to voluntarily seek membership with Sunkist as a result of competitive performance. As a result, Sunkist members had enjoyed both economies of scale and marketing strength.

But without a large volume base, Sunkist's marketing strength and pricing integrity were vulnerable. With less acreage in its membership, every component of Sunkist's carefully-constructed marketing program, every support service – sales operations, advertising, research – would become far more costly on a per-unit basis. Every Sunkist member would suffer.

"Frustration is an apt description because we know that so long as growers and shippers had choice, they voluntarily affiliated with Sunkist," the cooperative's president, Russell Hanlin, said at the time.

As industry competitors continued openly to declare their intent to expand by buying up land and packinghouses, Sunkist did some considerable soul searching. And out of its deep reckoning, the cooperative countered with a bold move of its own. Taking steps to insure that the risk associated with its new venture would pose no threat to the financial strength of either company, Sunkist and Fruit Growers Supply Company jointly capitalized a new subsidiary in January 1988: Sunkist Real Estate, Inc.

Sunkist Real Estate's primary business purpose was to provide real estate, financial and investment information services and short-term financing to Sunkist members and potential members. Its goal, obviously, was to attract additional citrus acreage and retain acreage already in the Sunkist system.

In its first 12 months of operation, the subsidiary financed for Sunkist members over 5,000 acres of additional citrus groves and a new packinghouse.

So successful was Sunkist Real Estate that by 1989, it had approved more than $36 million of property assistance loans. It had brought in more than 5,400 new acres to the Sunkist system, including the new packinghouse, and it had helped retain approximately 2,200 acres which likely would have been sold outside the system.

In the meantime, Sunkist had undertaken an intensive cost containment program to further reduce operations expenses. Fresh fruit marketing and advertising assessments decreased by 20 percent in 1988. By 1989, Sunkist had a net gain of nearly 7.5 million- carton equivalents in tree-crop volume.

While Sunkist Real Estate and the cooperative's cost-containing measures had helped Sunkist attract new members, there were other reasons backing Sunkist's renewed success. At the top of the list was Sunkist's financial strength. It had the best possible credit rating. In August 1989, Sunkist was the only U.S. agricultural cooperative retaining the A1+ and P-1 commercial paper ratings and a "double A" senior debt rating.

Sunkist had maintained these impressive ratings by taking steps not only to preserve its capital but to significantly reduce its borrowings. And it continued to earn profits by using its international business expertise and the value of the Sunkist trademark to pave the way into added-value, non-member products.

THE THREAT OF THE U.S. DOLLAR

Not all of Sunkist's challenges in the 1980s erupted on the home front. There was plenty going on overseas. The mighty U.S. dollar was rearing its head, and not to the advantage of American exporters. The stronger the dollar got, the more foreign currency it took to equal it, meaning U.S. goods were becoming more and more expensive for foreign buyers.

By 1983, the 40 percent strengthening of the U.S. dollar over European currencies had reduced Sunkist's trade there by four million cartons a year. The economic bankruptcy of the Eastern Bloc countries through the first half of the Eighties cost Sunkist millions of cartons of fresh fruit business each year. Europe's discriminatory duty against Sunkist also contributed to the decline.

HOLDING ONTO LEADERSHIP

Despite challenges abroad and pressures on the home front, Sunkist remained a stable force in the Far West citrus industry. By 1985, its revenues had reached the highest level ever at $837 million – a whopping increase of $81 million or nearly 11 percent over the previous season. That year, Sunkist had completed a co-generation plant, a joint venture with a partner who provided the capital. Providing a source for the production of both steam and electricity, the new facility would substantially reduce utility costs at Sunkist's Ontario plant.

Sunkist had also completed in 1985 the largest bulk frozen storage facility in the

SUNKIST DEFINED

"Sunkist Growers, Inc. is a nonstock membership cooperative marketing association representing citrus growers with orchards in California and Arizona.

Formed in 1893 as the Southern California Fruit Exchange, the organization was incorporated in 1905 as the California Fruit Growers Exchange.

The present name was adopted in 1952 to more closely identify the Company's operations with its world-famous trademark, SUNKIST.

The cooperative's principal business objectives are: to develop and maintain ready and reliable markets for members' fruit; to gain for member-growers the best possible return for their produce; and to supply consumers with readily available, top quality fresh citrus fruit and processed citrus products at reasonable prices.

Membership is limited to growers and cooperative associations of growers, and only persons engaged in the production of citrus fruit to be handled by Sunkist Growers, Inc. may serve on the Board of Directors.

The Board is the governing body of the marketing organization and has control of financial matters and other policies affecting the cooperative.

The Directors elect the President who is the chief executive officer to exercise general management control of the business and to provide leadership recommendations.

Sunkist's principal business activities are the sale of fresh oranges, lemons, grapefruit, and tangerines, and the manufacture and sale of processed citrus juice and peel products."

- Sunkist Growers, Inc., 1985

Built in 1985, this Sunkist facility in Ontario stores bulk frozen juice concentrates and is the largest in the western U.S.

western U.S. Not only did the storage facility allow the cooperative to greatly reduce the cost of handling frozen concentrated orange juice, but it would also allow Sunkist to become a very efficient user of Brazilian orange juice concentrate. Brazil had become the world's largest orange producer, although virtually all of its fruit was turned into processed products. The South American country was the world's dominant supplier of orange juice concentrate; in 1984 in the U.S. alone, Brazil had provided nearly half of the juice consumed by the American public.

Sunkist's new facility would allow it to receive tanker shiploads of Brazilian concentrate which would then be blended with its own members' juice to produce consistent quality and to supplement supply. Technological developments like these propelled Sunkist into a competitive position in the rapidly changing world of juice products.

In 1985, retiring chairman of the board, John V. Newman, made his last report, upholding his 54-year membership in the cooperative with a call for support.

"I have seen many changes in our business, but through all the years, one constant has been the steadying influence Sunkist has provided to the California-Arizona citrus industry," Newman said. "Acreage and production have fluctuated, and growers have had good years and bad years; but without Sunkist, many times our industry would have been in shambles."

Newman's successor would be Ralph E. Bodine of San Diego. Bodine had served on the boards of both Sunkist Growers and the Fruit Growers Supply Company since 1977. He was a second generation member of the Sunkist board, following in the steps of his father Arthur Bodine of Arizona. The new chairman was also a cum laude graduate of Princeton with a degree in economics.

Sunkist's strong marketing performance and its renewed membership recruitment program had allowed the cooperative to increase its share of growers and packinghouses. By 1985, the cooperative represented a slightly higher share of the industry than it did before the Blue Goose packinghouses had been purchased by a competitor.

Exports remained a powerful factor throughout the Eighties. Groundwork laid years earlier was paying off for Sunkist. An accord between the U.S. and Japan, initiated by private industry and government, had resulted in a progressive and dramatic expansion in Japan's orange quota – a quota which was moving up year after year.

The U.S. was providing 99 percent of that quota, with most of the fruit coming from California and Arizona. In 1986, Sunkist supplied more than 65 percent of that total, its best market share performance ever in Japan. That, coupled with a continuing strong performance in Hong Kong, Singapore, New Zealand, Australia, and Malaysia, resulted in a record-setting export year in 1986. Overseas shipments reached $232 million from the sale of over 20 million cartons of fruit.

San Diego's Ralph E. Bodine was chairman of Sunkist's board of directors from 1985-90.

Thomas N. Dungan, an Exeter, California grower, was elected chairman of Sunkist's board in 1990.

WORLD STATUS

With the close of the Eighties, Sunkist ranked among the ten largest cooperatives in America. Among the world's fruit and vegetable industry, it was the biggest. Of all the fresh citrus eaten in America, 65 percent came from California and Arizona, and Sunkist represented about 66 percent – or 6,500 – of those growers.

In an average year, Sunkist marketed about 68 million 40-pound cartons of fresh citrus fruit – 70 percent in the domestic market and 30 percent overseas. It was the largest shipper of fresh citrus fruit in America. Sunkist's principal foreign markets were Japan, Hong Kong, Southeast Asia, and Western Europe.

Additionally, about 800,000 tons of fruit were processed into a wide variety of juice and peel products.

The cooperative maintained 31 fully staffed sales offices in major metropolitan centers throughout the U.S. and Canada, and five overseas subsidiaries. The 150 men and women in these offices were local market experts. And they relied on Sunkist's computerized on-line system – a network of lines totaling 17,000 miles. Sales offices and shipping locations could communicate in print at 1,200 words per minute on everything from inventory data and sales inquiries to confirmations, manifests, and invoices.

In addition to its shipping expertise, Sunkist maintained its well-known name through advertising. And to further enhance its members' returns, the cooperative had helped launch new consumer products bearing its famous name. Through its licensed products program, Sunkist licensed technical know-how, proprietary ingredients, and its trademark to capable partners. That program brought in to Sunkist members several million dollars in royalty income each year. Licensed products bearing the Sunkist name had sales of nearly $1 billion in 1989. In fact, that year, Sunkist's soft drink royalties increased 79 percent, due in part to the efforts of the Sunkist licensee, Cadbury Schweppes, both at home and in capturing 18 percent of the United Kingdom orange carbonated soda market in less than one year.

The Eighties had been marked by shifting crop utilization, changes in membership and competition. But nearly every year had brought record-breaking revenues. Progressively more fresh fruit had been sold, while products fruits receipts had dropped. Cuts and decreases in operations, staffing, product lines and inventories had resulted.

In 1989, weather problems caused serious problems for citrus growers in the Far West. Sunkist initiated a cost-cutting program to help reduce operating expenses. But with Sunkist's centennial just a heartbeat away, everyone associated with the cooperative was excited about its future. Chairman Ralph Bodine, in his last report in 1989, expressed his excitement with, "This first hundred years is just a tune-up."

Lest Sunkist forget where its roots lay, however, Mother Nature would make its power felt not long after the Nineties opened.

SUNKIST'S POLICY MAKERS: THE BOARD OF DIRECTORS

Sunkist's directors are formally elected to one-year terms at the annual meeting in February of each year. The cooperative's bylaws require that a director be engaged in citrus production, although no rules specify the amount of acreage a director must represent. He or she may own under 40 acres or up to several thousand acres of citrus. Each director is elected from a district exchange to give direction to Sunkist. Directors attend monthly board meetings where management reports and operating recommendations are presented for their approval. The directors ratify appointment of all Sunkist officers, establish quality standards and grades for fresh fruit and products, and prescribe rules governing the use of trademarks, patents and copyrights of Sunkist Growers, Inc. Each director also serves on one or more board committees, established to advise on the operations of specific divisions of the cooperative.

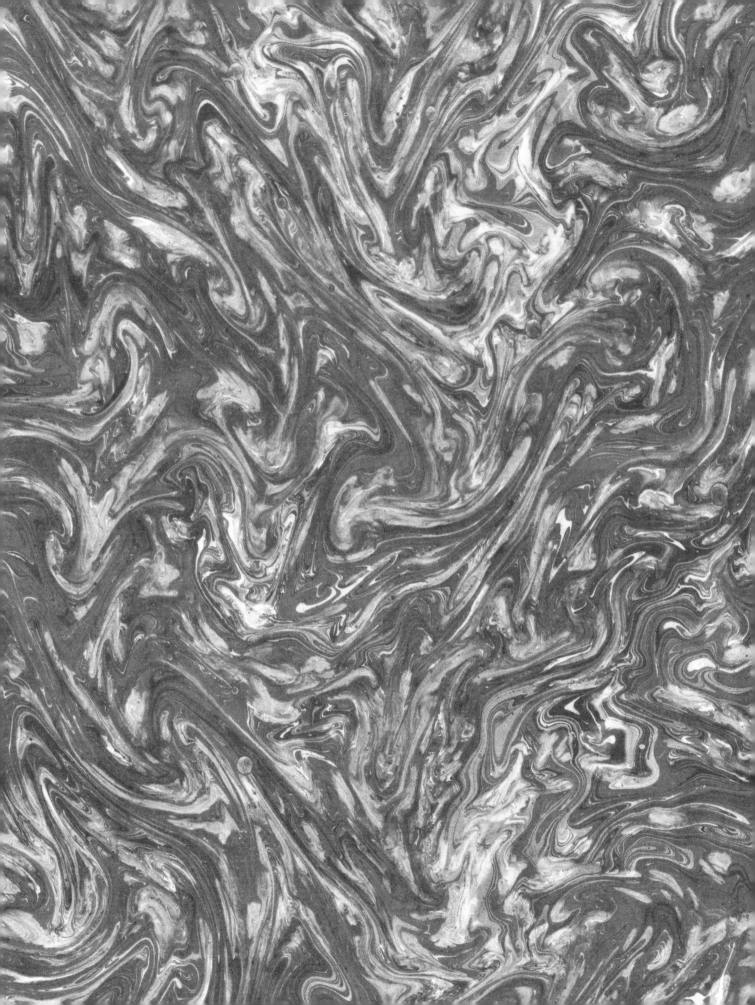

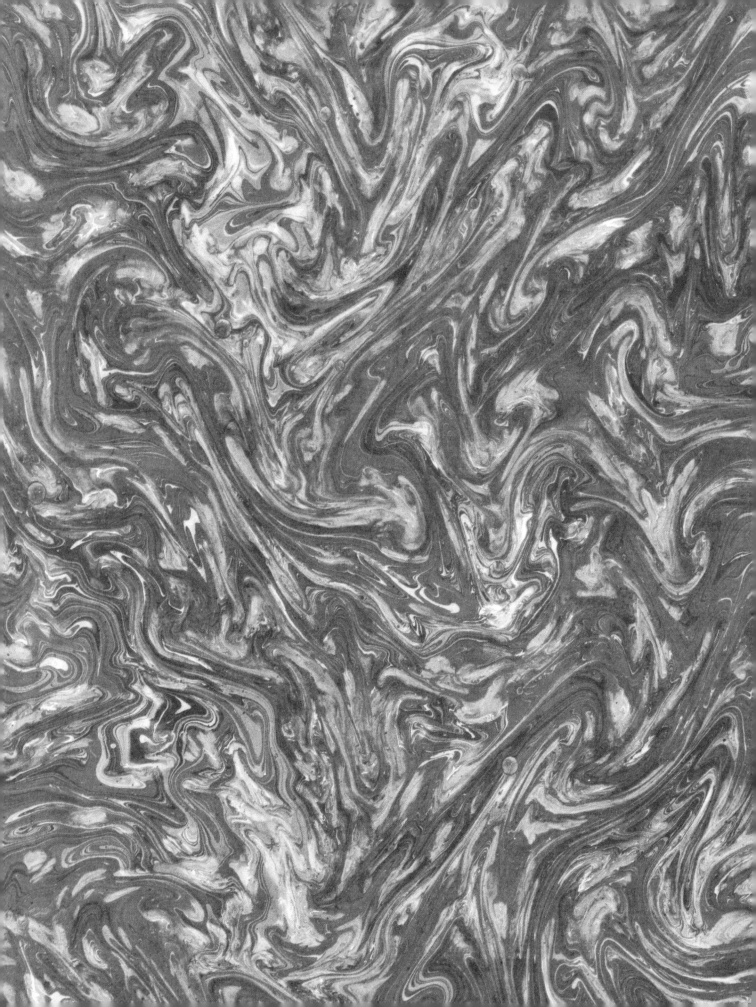

CHAPTER XI – The 1990s

STRONGER THAN EVER

The Christmas freeze of 1990 was the longest and coldest in California history. When it was over, not a single navel orange was left to market and the remaining citrus crops were reduced by half.

A change of Sunkist's board leadership marked the start of the Nineties, when Tom Dungan took over as chairman of the board from Ralph Bodine. Dungan, a graduate of Stanford University, was a fourth generation Sunkist grower from Tulare County, whose father had also served on Sunkist's board. For Dungan, the chairman's job gave him the opportunity to help guide a company he had literally grown up with.

Dungan's first year coincided with a banner year at Sunkist. In 1990, the cooperative celebrated a landmark in its history – its first billion-dollar year with record levels of revenue in both fresh domestic and export sales, as well as in products sales.

"More importantly," a proud Dungan reported to the Sunkist membership, "revenues from all sources back to you, the owners, are also at an all-time high of $795 million. This is an increase of 17 percent over last year and up 83 percent from just ten short years ago when I first joined the Sunkist board."

Fresh fruit shipments had reached a record high of 82 million cartons, while a whopping 788,000 tons of fruit had been processed into a variety of juice and peel products. That year, too, sales of Sunkist's licensed products had neared the $1 billion mark in gross revenues back to its licensees, offering a glimpse of what the ultimate value of the Sunkist trademark could someday be.

In 1990, another Medfly infestation had erupted, and against the "misinformed" outcries of "environmental zealots, political opportunists and an irresponsible press," according to Hanlin, the State of California had proceeded with aerial applications of malathion to eradicate the pest from California.

That year, too, an anti-agriculture initiative, "Big Green" or Proposition 126, had haunted California's farming sector, but had been dealt with victoriously for the state's farmers and agribusiness.

Sunkist had closed its books on the 1989-90 year. Two major citrus producers – Paramount Citrus and Sun Pacific – had signed into Sunkist membership, bringing 10 million cartons of fresh fruit volume and four packinghouses into the cooperative's system. President Hanlin had just finished writing his annual report letter to Sunkist's membership on December 5, 1990. With everything in place, it looked as if Sunkist and the western citrus industry were on top of the world.

Then, just a little more than two weeks later, disaster struck.

THE 1990 FREEZE

Beginning December 20, 1990, five consecutive nights of severe sub-freezing temperatures hit California as well Arizona. It was the longest, coldest freeze in California's history. Temperatures fell below freezing and stayed there, exceeding the record lows set in 1913. For ten nights, temperatures never rose above 26 degrees. The cold did not let up until January 3.

It seemed growers could do little to protect their crops. Wind machines, heaters, irrigation water, even helicopters to stir the air were no match for the cold. By the second night, even the fruit facing the orchard heaters froze. After that, growers wrote off the crop and worked simply to save their trees.

"Even the old-timers who remembered the big freezes of 1937 and 1949 had never seen anything like it," Hanlin reported. "No one could imagine a year when there was nothing, absolutely nothing, to harvest in the Valley."

The Christmas freeze left deep scars. The San Joaquin Valley was hardest hit. With 75 percent of its winter navel crop still on the trees and the summer crop of valencias just developing, the San Joaquin Valley's orange crops were wiped out. So were the lemons, the grapefruit, and the tangerines. Only a year before, the San Joaquin Valley had produced its biggest crop ever of navel oranges. When the cold finally departed, there was not a single navel orange remaining to market for 1991.

Fruit trees were damaged or killed. Growers would have no income for at least a year. Thousands of farm and packinghouse workers – valuable, long-time employees — were forced out of jobs. In some communities, unemployment rates exceeded 50 percent.

"It was trial by ice," Dungan noted. "The events of this year have brought home to us, as never before, the understanding of just how large a part the citrus industry plays in our lives – not just as growers but as members of the community."

Sunkist and the citrus industry would not forget the people victimized by the freeze. Hundreds of thousands of dollars were raised. Thousands of tons of food were donated. Sunkist, its growers, employees and affiliates contributed more than $400,000 to food banks. The industry pulled together to help its members survive until the next season. In Washington, D.C., Sunkist lobbied strongly to support legislation to extend unemployment benefits.

While almost all of the Southern California and Arizona citrus growing areas also were hit hard by the freeze, some 75 percent of the crops in those areas would survive with only moderate damage. They were to provide Sunkist its only supplies for 1991.

The 1990-91 freeze would be recorded as the third most costly disaster in California history, ranking behind the 1906 San Francisco and 1989 Loma Prieta earthquakes. For ten long months, the packinghouses in the San Joaquin Valley stood silent. In normal years, hundreds of thousands of cartons of fruit were harvested and packed daily. In 1991, vast storage areas held only pallets of donated foods awaiting delivery to hungry, unemployed workers.

SURVIVING THE FREEZE

In just a few short days, Sunkist's billion-dollar celebration had turned to concern. Its expected volume of 87 million cartons dropped to just 48 million – a level not seen in over ten

Sunkist did not forget the thousands of farm and packinghouse workers whose jobs ended with the freeze. Its growers, employees and affiliates contributed more than $400,000 to food banks.

For a short time after the freeze, some of the fruit could be processed for juice. Sunkist's two processing plants ran twenty-four hours a day, seven days a week, as long as there was salvageable fruit.

years. That loss of fruit would translate into an $18 million loss in company operating revenue for the fresh fruit side of the business alone. Fruit for processing declined by half. Immediately, Sunkist began devoting its attention to reducing operations and cutting expenses while retaining its fundamental capabilities.

Sunkist's budget was slashed from $41 million to $28 million. Programs and operations in every department of the company were reduced and jobs eliminated. Advertising and sales promotion programs were reduced by $7 million; administration and marketing expenses by $6 million.

The board deferred payment of $10 million of allocated non-member income to growers. This supplementary income was to be distributed only when total corporate equity exceeded requirements. "That position of strength was threatened by the freeze, and the postponement of the payment was another of the sad but necessary adjustments occasioned by the weather disaster," Hanlin reported.

Before the freeze, Sunkist's marketing and advertising assessment had been 50 cents per carton. After the freeze, it was 66 cents. Assessments were paid only by those who had fruit to sell. "Since growers who had fruit were earning much higher post-freeze prices and those who had no fruit paid nothing," Hanlin noted, "the increase was, fortunately, not a serious burden to anyone."

For a few short weeks after the freeze, some of the damaged fruit could be processed for juice, and Sunkist's processing plants ran three shifts a day, seven days a week, as long as the fruit was salvageable. Hundreds of trucks lined up at the plants in Ontario and Tipton as they waited six to eight hours to unload.

BATTLEFIELD OF MARKETING ORDERS

While Sunkist and its members were coping with the damage from the freeze, the cooperative found itself engaged in another costly and bitter battle over the continuation of the federal navel and valencia marketing orders.

A grower referendum was required every six years to guide the U.S. Secretary of Agriculture in determining whether the marketing orders should continue. Growers had always and overwhelmingly voted in favor of the orders, which allowed the citrus industry to maintain a steady supply of fruit to the marketplace while keeping prices in a relatively stable range.

In 1991, Sunkist's board of directors, strongly believing in marketing orders, exercised its right as a cooperative to cast, on behalf of its members, an association vote in favor of the continuation. They were encouraged in their positive vote by a large number of independent packinghouses. Yet, despite the referendum's affirmation of the marketing order, once again, "the usual opponents responded with law suits," Hanlin observed.

Marketing order battles would continue into Sunkist's 100th year. In December 1992, "anti-regulatory zealots in the Department of Agriculture and the White House – in their last month in office before a new Administration took over – arbitrarily suspended the navel and valencia marketing orders," Sunkist's Hanlin said. Suspended indefinitely, "these important marketing instruments are now left under a cloud," Hanlin said.

RECOVERY

Despite the trauma of the 1990 freeze, Sunkist and the industry would recover triumphantly. Because of high prices for the fruit that survived the freeze and the cooperative's astute marketing, Sunkist's total revenues for the 1990-91 season reached their second-highest figure ever at $956 million.

Sunkist was helped in its recovery by its diversification – one of its great strengths. Fifty percent of its volume originated in Southern California and Arizona; the other 50 percent in the San Joaquin Valley. Despite the devastation of the freeze, Sunkist still had significant quantities of fruit to sell.

Oddly enough, the setback reversed itself the very next season. The post-freeze crop yielded near-normal volumes of fruit.

A PLACE IN HISTORY

As 1991 edged into 1992, there was much more to consider. Sunkist was one of agriculture's success stories of the 20th century. It remained the largest citrus marketing cooperative in the world. Luck had played no role in making Sunkist the great company it had become.

Freeze or no freeze, Sunkist had the support of its 6,500 members – amounting to close to two-thirds of the citrus growers in the Far West. Together, they farmed 225,000 acres of navel oranges, valencia oranges, lemons, grapefruit, and tangerines. With the unique geographic make-up of California and Arizona, Sunkist growers could harvest fresh oranges, lemons and grapefruit every single day of the year.

As the cooperative readied itself for its centennial celebration, it still operated with the unique, interwoven system that had fueled Sunkist's success, a network nearly as old as Sunkist itself. It had its 28-member board of directors, each a grower committed to the success of Sunkist. There were 66 member packinghouses, which together packed 80 million 40-pound cartons of fresh citrus each year. There were 20 district exchanges acting as regional order fulfillment centers. There were the two state-of-the-art juice processing plants, one at Tipton, one at Ontario, capable of handling a million tons of citrus per year. They all helped Sunkist market its citrus, with some 70 percent going into fresh fruit channels and the other 30 percent into processing.

There was still the Fruit Growers Supply Company, providing equipment and supplies to growers and packinghouses at cost-effective prices. The Supply Company still owned and operated 350,000 acres of timberland in Northern California. No longer needed for making wooden packing crates, the timberlands were now operated on a sustained yield basis which provided Sunkist growers with several million dollars of supplementary income each year. Most importantly, the Supply Company produced most of Sunkist's fresh fruit cartons at its ultra-modern corrugated factory in Ontario, offering a vital and cost-effective service to members.

Millions of dollars more came from Sunkist's licensing agreements with its famous name. The cooperative continued to maintain the most extensive privately-owned citrus research laboratories in existence. Its vast marketing network was comprised of 31 fully staffed district sales offices, with more than 150 sales people, in major metropolitan areas throughout the U.S. and Canada.

Poised on the edge of the Pacific, Sunkist had a distinct transportation advantage with the growing Asian markets. Already, Japan was its largest overseas market, accounting for 20 percent of Sunkist's total revenues. As Korea, Taiwan, Thailand, Singapore, and Malaysia continued to increase their standards of living, Sunkist was already making inroads into markets there.

And through Sunkist's research and development division, the inventions continued to come. By 1992, one of the most exciting innovations involved fresh citrus fruit that was perfectly peeled by a revolutionary new process. The fruit remained absolutely fresh, with no preservatives. Properly handled, it had a shelf life of three weeks. For restaurants and mass feeding establishments, this development could provide citrus ready to eat with no additional labor and no peel to dispose of. It was revolutionary.

In 1992, Sunkist would mark another first: it began marketing pistachios. Part of Sunkist's strategy to capitalize on its unique ability to penetrate the perishable produce network in the U.S., the new venture was quickly effective. The pistachios, supplied by a Sunkist member who was the nation's largest producer of the nut, were marketed in produce sections of supermarkets all over the country. Not only did Sunkist gain from the marketing but earned royalties from the use of its trademark on the pistachio packaging.

But if, by 1992, any one development excited Sunkist, it was its new state-of-the-art computerized system. President Hanlin would call it "the landmark culmination of the century that will carry us into the next decade or two." Sunkist had invested $14 million into its new computer system, whose development budget Sunkist's board had held onto despite the 1990 freeze. An instantaneous domestic inventory/order processing system, it linked Sunkist's 66 packinghouses, 20 district exchanges, 31 district sales offices, and Sunkist Central.

The system would revolutionize Sunkist's operations, and new uses for it were regularly being discovered as 1993 arrived. The computer could tell instantaneously the floor count – by size and grade – of every carton of fruit in a Sunkist packinghouse. It could instantly gather estimates of fruit picking and packing operations to help Sunkist's sales staff in its high-pressure decisions. It could order, invoice, and interface directly with the computers of Sunkist's major customers. It dealt, not just in seconds, but in sub-second response time. No one else in the agricultural industry had anything like it.

"It will be a change in the culture perhaps equal in impact to the decline of the auctions in that we're going to have this massive information and response capability," Hanlin said.

As Sunkist entered its centennial year, the cooperative retained, above all, its hallmarks of high quality standards, face-to-face selling and its brand name. And it had the sound financial condition that was the envy of the entire agricultural community.

A proud Hanlin would reflect on the year of the killer freeze, and, on the eve of Sunkist's 100-year anniversary, he put into words his thoughts, a perspective that summed up everything the cooperative had weathered in its long and rich history.

"There are few industries and very few companies that can take a hit of that magnitude and make it through as well as Sunkist has," Hanlin reported. "The same dedication, persistence, intelligence and integrity that accomplished success for the Sunkist system also saw us through adversity and left us stronger. The Western citrus industry has recovered and Sunkist is ready to go forward."

So it had always been. And so it would always be.

THE END

Sunkist began its second one hundred years stronger than ever – with the same high quality standards, marketing network and world renown trademark that marked the success of the first one hundred Sunkist years.

Who would have believed in those first years that the cooperative would come this far, thought Hanlin, returning his gaze to Tokyo's distant horizon. Sunkist's roots go back over a hundred years, he reflected, yet it's kept ever young by the new blood of its people, the innovative strides of its research, the abiding appeal of its fruit, and the undying truths of its cooperative principles.

And, the executive thought, there was that one-in-a-million name: Sunkist. Ageless, treasured, a part of American culture. It conjured up values people could still feel with a sense of pride. It spoke of a lasting heritage, a legacy of success. And it proved, Hanlin thought as he turned away to meet with his Japanese customers, all this was possible when people chose to unite for all the best reasons.

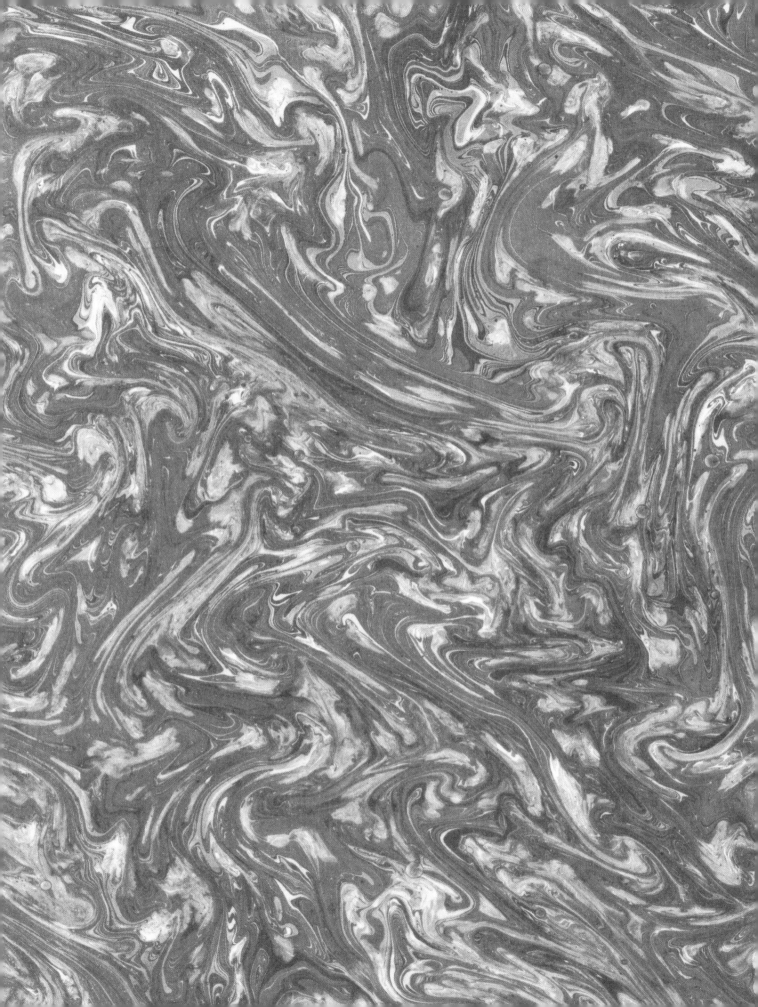

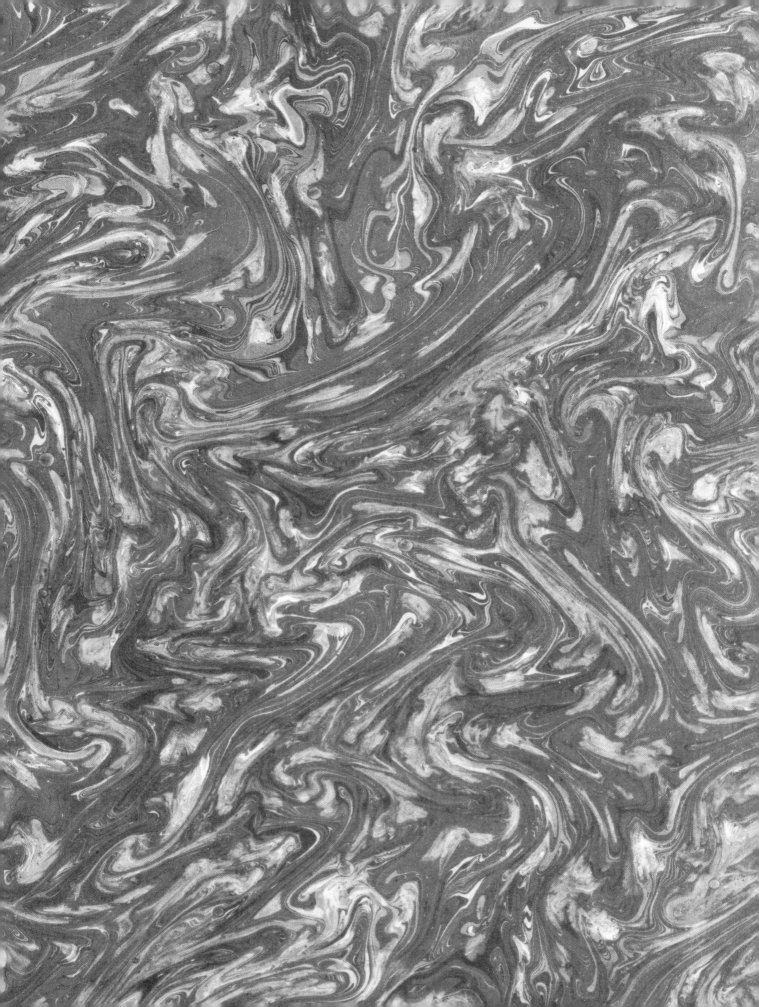

Project Coordinator: Claire H. Peters
Author: Catherine Merlo
Book Design & Graphics: M. Jack Cullimore
Photo-typesetting: Candice S. Garnand

Sunkist wishes to credit the following for their invaluable contributions to this history:

Rahno Mabel MacCurdy
The History of the California Fruit Growers Exchange, 1925

Irwin W. Rust and Kelsey B. Gardner
Sunkist Growers, Inc.
A California Adventure in Agricultural Cooperation, Farmer Cooperative Service, USDA, 1960

C.H. Kirkman, Jr.
The Sunkist Adventure, Farmer Cooperative Service, USDA, 1975

Ed Ainsworth
Journey With The Sun, 1968

C.C. Teague
Ten Talks On Citrus Marketing, 1939

C.C. Teague
Fifty Years A Rancher, 1944

Albert Meyer
History of the California Fruit Growers Exchange - 1893-1920, 1950

Walton Bean
California: An Interpretive History, 1973

Pomona Centennial-Bicenntenial Committee, Publisher
Pomona Centennial History, 1976

Gordon T. McClelland and Jay Fast
California Orange Box Labels: An Illustrated History, 1985

CREDITS

Russell Hanlin
President, Sunkist Growers, Inc.

Curt Anderson
Vice President, Member and Public Relations, Sunkist Growers, Inc.

C. Chris Martinez
Records Systems Supervisor, Sunkist Growers, Inc.

Velma Pontius
Public Relations Secretary, Sunkist Growers, Inc.

Millard Beemer
former Sunkist director, Pauma Valley, California

John Newman
former Sunkist chairman of the board, Ventura, California

Jack Dickenson
Limoneira Company, Santa Paula, California

Betsy Blanchard Chess
Limoneira Company, Santa Paula, California

Judy Harpster
Limoneira Company, Santa Paula, California

Dorcus Thille
Santa Paula, California

Mr. and Mrs. Robert Hardison
Santa Paula, California

Ernest H. Bowman
former Sunkist employee, videotaped interview, 1990

Francis Johnson
former Sunkist employee, videotaped interview, 1989

Alfrida Teague
widow of Milton Teague, videotaped interview, 1990

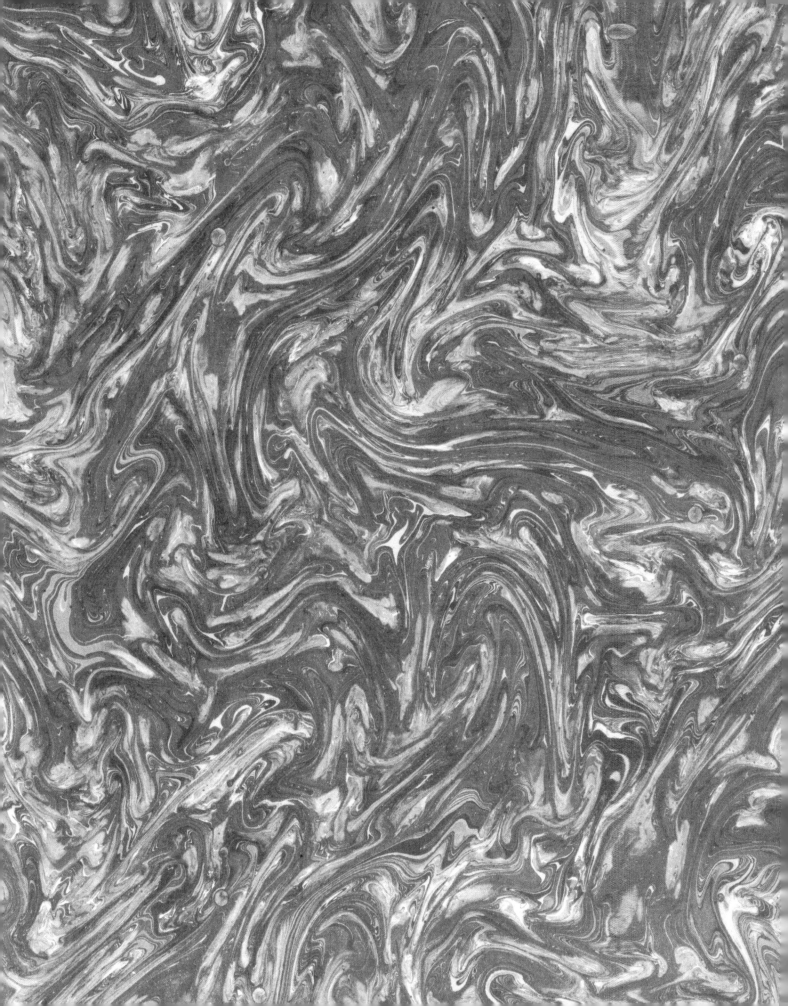

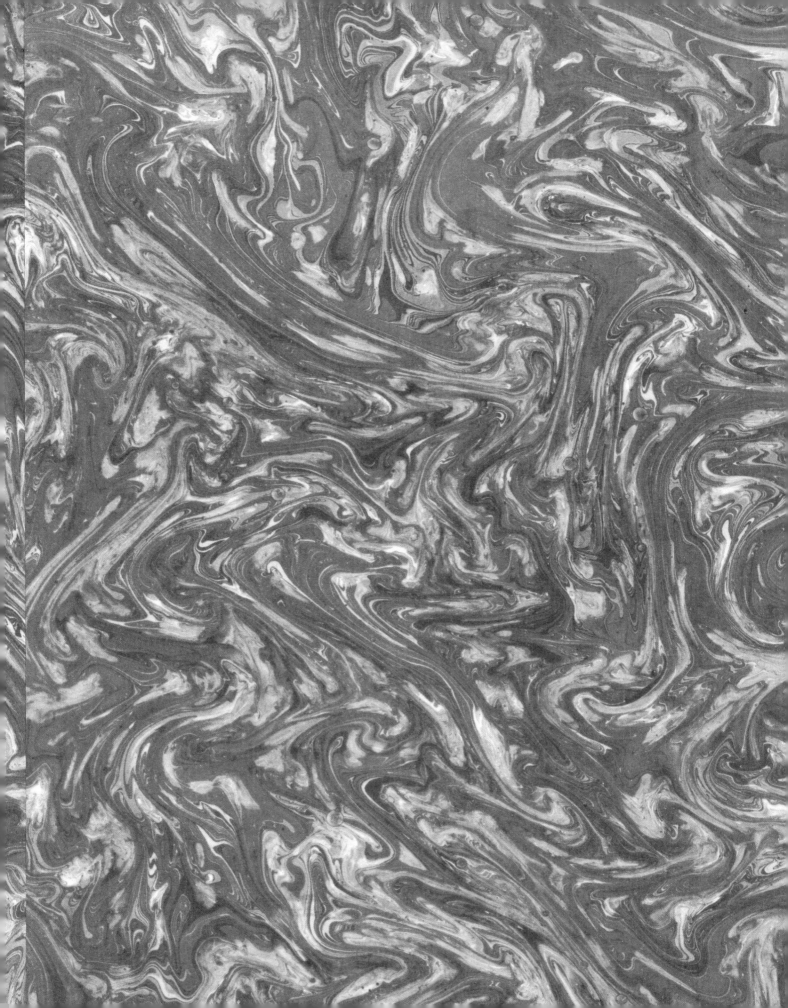